MARTIAL *(Marcus Valerius Martialis) was born in Spain in the year 40 A.D., or thereabout. His parents were Roman citizens, and his early schooling acquainted Martial with the works of classical antiquity from Homer to Virgil. At the age of twenty-four, he traveled to Rome, where he began moving in a literary circle headed by Lucan and Seneca, both of whom were also of Spanish birth. Soon Martial was making a modest living as a composer of short, pithy verse whose main purpose was to delight the wealthy and politically powerful Romans who were his patrons. The patron-client system affected Martial's works as it affected all the literature of his day, and while he was a cynical and astute observer of Roman society and its ills, Martial's art was tailored to flatter his patrons and to assure his protection at the imperial court. Although his epigrammatic poetry was, generally speaking, neither heroic in subject matter nor philosophically profound, Martial's sardonic and ribald wit, his disdain for hypocrisy — whether sexual or political — and his stunning, rapier-like mode of poetic expression gained him great popularity both among his fellow poets and the patrons for whom he labored. The last decade or so of his life was spent in retirement, during which time he looked back proudly on his two major achievements: his body of work — more than a thousand finely honed epigrammatic poems, and the simple fact that he had survived as an artist within the dictatorial and capriciously cruel Roman society. Martial died in Spain in 104 A.D.*

EPIGRAMS
OF
MARTIAL

NEWLY TRANSLATED
AND WITH AN INTRODUCTION BY
Palmer Bovie

A PLUME BOOK from
NEW AMERICAN LIBRARY
TIMES MIRROR
New York, Toronto and London

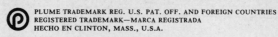

PLUME TRADEMARK REG. U.S. PAT. OFF. AND FOREIGN COUNTRIES
REGISTERED TRADEMARK—MARCA REGISTRADA
HECHO EN CLINTON, MASS., U.S.A.

SIGNET, SIGNET CLASSICS, MENTOR AND PLUME BOOKS
are published *in the United States* by
The New American Library, Inc.,
1301 Avenue of the Americas, New York, New York 10019,
in Canada by The New American Library of Canada Limited,
295 King Street East, Toronto 2, Ontario,
in the United Kingdom by The New English Library Limited,
Barnard's Inn, Holborn, London, E.C. 1, England

FIRST PRINTING, SEPTEMBER, 1970

Printed in the United States of America

quod tegitur maius creditur esse malum

CONTENTS

INTRODUCTION

Marcus Valerius Martial was born in Spain around 40 A.D. at Bilbilis, near Saragossa (Caesar Augusta). His parents, Roman citizens living in the Western province, conferred the common praenomen Marcus on their son and added the cognomen Martialis to signify that he was born on the first of March—a day Martial likes to remind himself of in his unmartial epigrams. The nomen Valerius is also a conventional Roman family name, which some scholars conjecture Martial assumed after he became a poet, to associate his work with that of Catullus, to whom he feels closely related as an artist. After his early years and first schooling in Spain—in the course of which he acquired a wide familiarity with the Classics from Homer to Virgil and a sensitivity to the meters and styles of the lyric poets—Martial went to Rome, at the age of 24, and was introduced into the circle of Spanish friends there. It was only a year later that two of these friends, Seneca and the young poet Lucan, were executed for conspiring against Nero. Martial felt the reverberations of political reality at the outset of his efforts to enjoy a career in the glamorous metropolis.

Martial's first sixteen years in imperial Rome have been characterized as years of "poverty-stricken dependence on patrons not overgenerous in return for the complimentary verses he addressed to them." The patron and client system affected literature as well as civil life, and during the sensational last years of Nero's reign, as well as under the later emperors, Martial sought influence and protection at the court and among powerful friends of high social and professional standing, like his compatriots Decian and Quintilian or his namesake Julius Martial, or Pliny. During these three decades from 64 until some time after 96 when he returned to Spain and retired from city life, the poet geared his behavior to the political and social machinery of the metropolis. Under Vespasian's son Titus he won the privilege of rank in the equestrian order with the slight measure of financial security it afforded. When Domitian became emperor after Titus' death in 81, Martial strenuously courted the new ruler, and gained his attention and approval by addressing a number of flattering epigrams to him. The first seven years of Domitian's reign augured well for Rome and seemed to be carrying forward the strong and practical administrative programs inaugurated by Vespasian's responsible style of government. But from 88 on Domitian became more and more autocratic until, obsessed by the fear of assassination, he embarked on the "terror" of 93–96. Martial like others could only wait and see if events would repeat the grim pattern of Nero's end. After Domitian's assassination Martial like others acclaimed the accession of Nerva, whose 16 months of rule were distinguished by a return to political sanity, chiefly important for legislation that directly aided the poor and underprivileged in Rome and Italy. Nerva's choice of Trajan as his successor, who ran the Empire exceptionally well from 98 until his death in 117, also brought the first Spanish provincial citizen to the highest seat of power.[1]

A well-educated provincial from the middle of nowhere, Martial might have turned out to be one of those parasites and scroungers he describes in his epigrams, a courtier, a social hanger-on, a harmless and unexceptionable cliff dweller with good "contacts"; he might have pursued the profession of law with its busy demands for activity in the Forum and in the

---

[1] Trajan was the son of M. Ulpius and a Spanish mother. He was born at Italica in Baetica on 18 Sept. 53 A.D. The second Spanish Roman emperor was Hadrian (117–138 A.D.), the son of P. Aelius Hadrianus Afer and Domitia Paulina of Gades (Cadiz). He was also born at Italica, in 76 A.D.

courts, or have adapted the skill in rhetoric absorbed in his literary training to the opportunities for public speaking and recitations then very much in vogue. All of these matters he has some direct experience of and uses as subjects in his epigrams. Quintilian made a lofty career in his appointment as the first Imperial Professor of Literature, and Pliny was a tasteful amateur of letters: both were eminent public figures whose interest and affection Martial can claim. Addressing Quintilian in the ninetieth epigram of Book II, Martial is somewhat apologetic about not being willing to "do" more with his life at Rome, and rather ruefully considers the fact that he has years of "work" in him but doesn't seem to be applying himself. For a variety of reasons he chose the precarious existence of the artist's life, as if by a combination of social instinct and intellectual training his knowledge of literature had brought him to the point of resolving to do something with the art of poetry. Whatever motives, attractions and disinclinations led him to this point of pursuing his own objects through the medium of poetry, he did gain self-realization in the act of writing, and came to savor the astringent sense of being admired and envied, read, quoted, and plagiarized, of being famous and notorious, of circulating as a poet of unusual and original powers. When he retired to Spain at the end of his career, he could look back and laugh at the curiously happy fate which balanced sixteen bright and full years of literary recognition against the sixteen blank years of "poverty-stricken dependence on patrons" and accept the hard cushion of rural isolation as a healthy if uncouth reward for meeting and beating the competition in the fashionable, dictatorial, expensive capital of civilization.[2]

What he made of himself, what he "did," his "work," is

---

[2] Not without a pang of regret: "I miss that audience of my fellow-citizens to which I had grown accustomed, and seem to myself a pleader in a strange court; for whatever is popular in my small books my hearer inspired. That subtlety of judgment, that inspiration of the subject, the libraries, theatres, meeting-places, where pleasure is a student without knowing it—to sum up all, those things which fastidiously I deserted I regret, like one desolate." Prefatory epistle to Book XII, [Loeb, II, p. 317, trans. by Ker].

made clear enough to us from his poems all written in clear, concrete Latin verse, predominantly in the eleven-syllable form favored by Catullus, in the senarius (the six-beat iambic line) favored by the comic poets, or the elegiac couplet favored by Propertius and Ovid. He chose to adapt the traditional forms of certain kinds of verse to his own new purposes and persisted in perfecting the medium of expression he had hit upon. He veered away from large commitments although he has the utmost regard for Virgil and can heartily congratulate his contemporary Silius Italicus for working on the epic scale. He deplores the unreality factor in mythology and when he does employ figures from this illusionary realm of the imagination, he reduces them to the psychological dimensions of human personality. He steers clear of anything large, long, or grand. In a sense, then, Martial's whole art is a way of confining reality to man's perception of it, of cutting experience down to size—in his poems he wants to arrive at the irreducible individual. It is not the vast architecture or the elevating or incomprehensible purpose of the Cathedral that interests him, but the statues niched into place lower down. Like a Pygmalion he falls inadvertently in love with the statues and wants to revive them and, unlike Pygmalion, to make fun of them because they are not godlike.

It was this crafty way of getting a grasp on his fellow man that must have urged Martial to experiment with his epigrams during the early years in Rome. When the Colosseum was dedicated by Titus in 80 A.D. the poet was ready with a group of poems about it—thirty-three of which editors today assign to this initial book, the *liber spectaculorum*. I presume that there were hundreds behind these, which Martial wrote and tried out on his friends and enemies, of which the *liber spectaculorum* is a special batch with a certain slant on a certain event. Like the other collections of epigrams in the individual books he subsequently produced, the ones we still have and read are the distilled result of his craft of trial and error in carving some well-outlined experience into a form demanding grace and dexterity. The modern reader may be put off by these first epigrams, mainly because Martial's point of view in the *liber spectaculorum* is not as clear as we expect it to be. In the canonical twelve books of the epigrams proper we are always made aware of the author's point of view, the stance in which he writes the poem, but here we find him rather non-committal, or indulging in easy acceptance of the facts he is decorating with verbal colors, or evincing an unguarded enthusiasm for the great event. He reacts too much like a spectator at the games, awed, impressed, nearly stunned by the display, greedily feasting his eyes on the extravaganza. Selected gruesome views are shown, through anecdotes or descriptions, or there is too much panorama: we don't quite know what to make of it. Could Martial have approved of the gladiatorial mess, even when two champions fight to a standstill and are saved from exhaustion and death only by the gracious signal from the Emperor? Is it all right for a criminal to be strung up on a flying machine and then dropped sloppily to death on the arena floor like a Daedalus who was all thumbs? Even we know that it wasn't *Daedalus'* wings which failed. When the Roman establishment diverts a clamoring mob of 45,000 spectators by performing the drama of Daedalus with a real live criminal under capital sentence, why isn't Martial horrified? Or when another victim, in the guise of Orpheus, is paced through the story of the poet only to be gobbled up by a bear released through a trapdoor in the arena floor, how can Martial bring himself to say that Eurydice must have been in a hurry to get her bard back? Doesn't he sense the innate cruelty of this show as well as its variance from the literary tradition of the myth? If an actual condemned robber Laureolus had once been crucified and torn to pieces by wild beasts, years back, was it equally sensational to work this out again in the Flavian Amphitheater to make a more modern Prometheus?

When he rehearses some of the animal acts we begin to look with the fascinated eye that Martial uses so expertly in the later epigrams. Seeing the grotesque justice of a rhinoceros or an elephant goring a bull, the poet dwells momentarily on the massively tapered point of that act of vengeance. The trained tigress who goes on a rampage and mangles a lion added a new dimension to her native ferocity when she left the African jungle for the Flavian Amphitheater. A lion who mauls his trainer, however, and is cut down by the ring attendants' spears, merely failed to learn the first and last lesson of the Roman world: obedience to the ruler. The elephant kneeling in the sand in front of the emperor's box, the wild doe halting there and gazing at the emperor, momentarily immune from attack, animate the idea that Rome has brought all things under the sway of its sacred superior power. In the first book of the epigrams Martial recurs to some of the animal acts, in particular to the cute trick of training a rabbit to hop in and out of a lion's mouth unmolested; the poet seems compelled to devote several epigrams to this, obsessed by the game. It is a strange little event and you wonder if the Colosseum was constructed for such fluff and bluff. Probably not, but suppose that an individual spectator, or hundreds or thousands among the 45,000 ticket-holding members of the audience, identified his safe seat with that rabbit's amazing perch; or imagine a saucy, opinionated poet trying to go his own way but subject to the whims of an autocratic court and to the approval of temperamental patrons: we have a picture of that charming miracle, social anxiety.

In the *Book of the Games* Martial finds no field for denuncia-tion—omitting reference to the slaughter of 5,000 beasts on the opening day, for example—and embraces with excited enthusiasm the revelation of the eighth wonder of the world. He registers no disgust at the cruelty and malice afoot, no sympathy with the victims underfoot but stresses the glamour of progress constructed here for the pleasure of the populace. But even at the first stage in his poetry he captures the views, imprisms the captives as well as the throngs and the building itself; and with naturalistic rendering develops and prints unfading pictures of the grandeur that was Rome. When he takes a day off it turns into a veritable Roman Holiday. He watches the show before he comes to grips with the art of concentrating on the spectators.

Four or five years later Martial produced two new collec-tions of light verse in the form of epigrammatic couplets written to accompany presents given at the Saturnalia (the winter holiday from December 17 to 23). Like the verses composed for the Colosseum, the *Xenia* ("Gifts for guests") and *Apophoreta* ("Gifts for guests to take home") are mere pendants, dwarfed by the object they describe or comment on. The poetic statement, the thought about the thing, is scaled down to microcosmic proportions. Of course, a greeting card to go with a toothpick is hardly overshadowed. Or, in sending a friend off with fine small-size note paper ("Vitellian tablets") or with a few sheets of larger paper, you spare him boredom simply by providing him with blank pages. A marble statue of Leander would far outweigh its greeting card, but Martial's romantic sentiment keeps the thought afloat ("Drown me on the way back"). A copy of Virgil makes Martial think of how small a parchment can contain the "mighty Maro," and even bear his features on the cover. For, "Propertius in a single volume," Martial tags the gift with the thought of the poet's inspiring mistress: Propertius made Cynthia famous, but she made him famous. So throughout the *Apophoreta* gifts of different sorts and sizes are assigned the uniform label of couplet wherein the thing assumes the added luster of an amusing if unexceptionable idea about it. The eleven-syllable lines accompanying the gift of a bedroom lamp are a glowing tribute to silence:

> Dulcis conscia lectuli lucerna,
> quidquid vis facias licet, tacebo.

> A lamp am I, aware of your joy in bed:
> Do what you will: not one word will be said.
> (39: Lucerna Cubicularis)

Each present is reduced to a couplet describing it, and the verses are compressed to a one- or two-word title. Martial reminds his readers that they can deal with him briskly. If they don't want to plough through the whole couplet, they can just read the title and, learning what it's about, skip over if the subject doesn't appeal. Or, in the preface to the *Xenia* volume, he reminds the reader that the whole book costs only four sesterces: he can probably get it for half-price from the bookseller Tryphon, who will still make a profit. Besides, if the reader is as short of cash as the poet (*si tibi tam rarus quam mihi nummus erit*), he can send the greeting card instead of a gift.

With a curious concentration on the minute dimensions of his art Martial again managed to catch the public eye, in these apparently frivolous performances after years of experimenting with things he saw through his poetic lenses. I presume that he discarded a great deal, tried out a vast number of these trifles on friends and strangers, in the tedious process of waiting for them to catch on. And the same must be true for the epigrams proper, the twelve books of which began to be issued from 85 on, every year or so, until 101 or 102. To bring the poems together in enough quantity for a volume of around a hundred meant selecting from the bulk of many that may have caught on momentarily, those that promised to hang on and to endure rereading because of their crafty elegance, their subject matter, or the idea expressed. In Book I of the epigrams Martial mentions a collection of his "early work" made by his friend Valerianus, which he feels he has long since surpassed. The *Xenia* and *Apophoreta* show the strides Martial has made since he began composing minor poems for the pleasure of the populace. In the *Book of the Games* he was an ideal spectator subject to but not entirely carried away by his enthusiasm for the novel territory being explored by the government for the mass communication of pleasure. Like the emperors and their people he was no emotional weakling, but capable of devouring the spectacle as one in the anonymous throng. Now, in the "gift" poems, the conspicuous display of generosity becomes individual and private. Formerly he was capable of only a few guarded comments on the whole scene. Now, with practice, and after closer familiarity with the social instincts of his world, Martial modestly expropriates the expropriators. He has no gifts to send but the gift of words—it is enough for him in the developing strength of his art to comment on things: this is the liberty he takes at the Saturnalia.

We acquire information about private tastes and behavior when we flip through the pages of the *Xenia* and *Apophoreta* again—just as from the *liber spectaculorum* we gain some knowledge of what the contests and shows in the arena actually were—it is somewhat like reading advertisements or scanning an anthology of menus to skim through these couplets that limn the desirable items on the social and gastronomic agenda of Roman society: an enticing array of things, an inconsequential Capitalist Manifesto.[3] The *Xenia* shows us what the Romans liked to eat or, on special occasions like the Saturnalia, to savor, and Martial's list of 127 place-gifts culled no doubt from the many more he had fabricated take us on a guided tour of the greater intestine. From pepper and spice, barley, lettuce, figs and quince, on to damsons, apples, and exotic fruit, not omitting either lowly but useful raisins and the "early" Persian peach, or apricot (*Persica praecocia*). Cheeses and sausages of many sorts and varieties clamor for attention and a bright remark if possible, if not a grand illusion—(*Lucanian Sausages*: "Daughter of a Picenian sow, here I come . . ."). Or from cheese we go back to milk, with an order of beestings, veer off among eggs, and arrive at the transformed barnyard of plucked fowl: a beccafico, duck, and, perhaps by association, goose-liver, not to mention the grander size for: swan, flamingo, peacock. For venison there is no end of choice among stag, hare, the milk-foal of the wild ass—somewhere earlier, sleepy dormice make an appearance—and doe, oryx (antelope?), gazelle. The victuals are flourished brightly, the list swelled by the varieties of fish course and the choices of wine. And the sumptuous record of feasting ends with a card accompanying a crown of roses, like some grace beyond the reach of the culinary art.

In the *Apophoreta* the eye lights on a different list of objects: writing paper, tablets, note paper, parchment, pens, a styluscase. Martial begins his list with the materials that make it possible at all. He continues with a random catalogue of possessions: oil lamps, candelabra, tapers, candles; toothpaste,

---

[3] Erst kommt die Moral, dann kommt das Fressen!

a toothpick, an earpick; hats, sunshades, a parasol. Metal gleams from an array of knives, daggers and swords, but softer tones are felt from gifts of slippers, hats, brassieres, girdles. A flute is one thing, pet birds another: parrot, nightingale, magpie. A falcon is sent along as a bird-catcher, but also a decoy bird at the end of a limber cane pole. We read of book-cases, combs, soap; a set of whips (for use on schoolboys, but not to be opened for five days). Tables of citrus wood are highly praised in polished verse and tables of mere maple, without the fine grain of lemonwood, held up as perhaps just as adequate. The alternation of cards for an expensive gift and an inexpensive one, as in the two kinds of table, fulfills the intention announced at the head of the book of *Apophoreta*:

> While Senators rejoice in dinner dress, and our Emperor wears the freedom cap and the house slave is not afraid to look the Aedile in the face . . . receive these lots in which gifts of rich and poor alternate; let everyone give his own guest his proper prize.

Surely some minute social scruple, some blend of sardonic acceptance and sympathetic wonder attaches to that clever contrast between expensive gifts and cheap gifts Martial insists upon in his arrangement. Generosity can take two forms. But the bulk of the book goes on; after the tables we read of cups, chalices, goblets, tankards, flasks, or flagons for iced water. Then the verses address themselves to clothes, warm outer woolens, togas, and cloaks, mantles, and tunics. There are playthings, volleyballs and exercise balls of different kinds, a guitar, and then art objects, especially statues, in gold, silver, terracotta, and marble. Among animals we single out a pair of mules, a jennet, a trick dog; and among slaves—surely not one of the poor man's gifts—we discover a caterer: *Opsonator*— here he is, your caterer, merely tell him what you want for dinner and it's as good as prepared for you. A thoughtful item on the agenda of conspicuous consumption. Another gift slave is a shorthand writer:

Notarius

Currant verba licet manus est velocior illis
nondum lingua suum dextra peregit opus.

Dictate fast as you will, their hand is faster still:
The tongue hasn't yet done when the hand is through.

These verses about the secretary make it look as if he was capable of anticipating the words he was taking down in shorthand. But it probably refers chiefly to the rapid copying accomplished by the learned slave scribes, as Ker observes:

> This epigram explains the small price at which Martial's poems could be sold by Tryphon. A number of slaves as short-hand writers could copy books cheaply.
>
> (Loeb, II.512)

And of course the *Apophoreta* is itself a kind of literary flourish, reinforced with its awareness of famous books as good gifts — a Homer, a Menander, a Cicero; copies, expensively bound, or in simple wrappings, of Virgil, Propertius, Livy (we'd give a fortune for that complete edition of Livy's history today), of Sallust (whose high place among historians Martial recognizes); little volumes of Ovid, Tibullus, Catullus, and Lucan. The appearance of such objects among the 123 entries of the *Apophoreta* sets the stage neatly for the appearance of the first two collections of epigrams, which were issued in book form at the same time and both together around the end of 84. In subsequent editions, Books I and II were published separately, as Martial went on to accumulate more and more epigrams. Book III came out in 87 or 88 while he was in France, "Gallia Togata," on some semiofficial tour of duty in the guise of his rank as tribune. Book IV appeared at the end of 88, Book V in 89, VI in 90, VII in 92. VIII, with is florid dedication to Domitian and its toned-down and conservative array of epigrams, came out in 93, during the first stages of the "terror." Martial revisited Bilbilis several times and by 101, when the last book of epigrams appears, is firmly settled there in retirement from Rome, comfortably established in a villa given to him by an appreciative Spanish lady, Marcella.

In translating the first four books of Martial's epigrams, I hope to acquaint the reader again with Martial's representative views of civilized life and behavior during the decades when Rome was progressing through the first proud stages of her imperial glory. The poet looks at the life swirling around him and, taking the measure of its difficulties and delights, finds his subject there, becoming the critic as well as the advocate of the life he knows best. Martial is not a satirist, but a lyric poet, a minor poet who wrote verse that constituted a major tour de force. He worked on a small scale deliberately, but so prolifically as to produce as much as an epic bard. At the end of Book IV he reminds himself and us that a vast lot of epigrams are perhaps more than enough for the sophisticated reader to keep on appreciating indefinitely. So he will desist. But he is back again next year, at the Saturnalia, with another batch of presents, slices of life for that discerning connoisseur, the Roman citizen, urbane, sensitive, ribald. Clearly, the artist working in a traditional form as old as epitaphs or graffiti has found his medium, attuned his lyric voice, and sharpened his perceptive vision on—his fellow man and environs. He can admit to being notorious for pinning down his fellow creatures on paper.

Each of the separate books of the Epigrams offers much the same variety of events, anecdotes, caricatures, line drawings, descriptions. I have translated four books entire and unexpurgated to show the uniformity as well as the variations within the kaleidoscopic field of an annual Martial collection. I have selected other epigrams from the remaining books to preserve the continuity as well as range of Martial's commentary. It is hardly necessary to analyze the implications of his poetry, for the implications are really explications—there is no subtle afterthought or suggestive quality to construe further about what he means. To that degree he is eminently clear and fair in setting before us the life he breathes, and sighs over, and delights in.

As for the style, the main meters he favors confine the verse to a traditional neatness and brevity and dictate a compressed force that, once mastered, functions with ease and aplomb. The epigram lets the reader off quickly, it tries not to let him down. It doesn't raise him up either, being an unelevated and plainspoken art of words. But it hopes to leave him with a memorable picture of events, or profile of a person, or the sensuous feel of some prized thing. Being an art of statement as well as of description, Martial's epigram often pulls a logical rug out from under its subject's feet: you do this so we can admire you? Then we know you're vain. Or the lines list a series of compliments, only to end with a single, poised insult. Sometimes painted in lush colors, sometimes etched in acid, these kind and unkind epigrams reflect their meanings in a sensuous and clearly limned form. We see that the "Martial collection" is in book form a kind of grouping that the artist himself arrived at, for he will run through several views of the same kind of thing, as if he were writing an epigram by direct association with another, before he veers off on a different tack. In mild effrontery to the form itself, he every now and then extends it deliberately, and writes long epigrams. These are usually pastoral ballads in which he descants upon the bliss and pseudograce of life in nature, which he may then offset with a drawn-out paean to the bewildering edginess of city life. Even the long epigrams end quickly, and as a translator and student of Martial's work I hardly need go on at length about the quality and serviceability of his poetry. Pliny wrote rather condescendingly but with sincere admiration about the result of Martial's efforts:

I have just heard of the death of poor Martial[4], which much concerns me. He was a man of acute genius, and his writings abound in both wit and satire, combined with equal candour. When he left Rome I complimented him by a present to defray the charges of his journey, in return for the little poem which he had written about me. . . . Do you not think that the poet who wrote in such terms of me, deserved some friendly marks of my bounty then, and that he merits my sorrow now? For he

[4] Martial's death in 104 is dated by this reference in Pliny's letter.

gave me the most he could, and it was want of power only, if his present was not more valuable. But to say truth, what higher can be conferred on man than fame, and applause, and immortality? And though it should be granted, that his poems will not be immortal, still, no doubt, he composed them upon the contrary supposition.

Literary tradition has somewhat belied this verdict in so far as Martial's poems have enjoyed a more fashionable afterlife, exerted more influence, and held more appeal for later readers than the writings of the gentle and gentlemanly advisor to Trajan. To describe the particular force of Martial's word-wielding, I would rather rely on the suggestion made by Vladimir Nabokov:

> There is, it would seem, in the dimensional scale of the world, a kind of delicate meeting place between imagination and knowledge, a point arrived at by diminishing large things and enlarging small ones, that is intrinsically artistic.
>
> *Speak, Memory,* p. 122

This possibility allows for Martial, if it does not account for him. At a time when Rome was gorging itself on grandeur, Martial went on an aesthetic diet, by reducing a poem to a thought. He experimented with disillusion. He put on the armor of sales resistance. His cynical, conversational realism apparently made him enemies—of the sort he felt it was worth making.

His outrageous sexual candor has a point, for the subject is one that cannot be healthily disregarded or happily exaggerated. As for the obscenity of a small part of his work, Martial is frank to avow it and deliberate in adopting the language of lyric (as in Catullus) or satire, for his epigrammatic ends. As with food, money, politics, clothes, religion, business, and the professions, the avocation of sex is a complex human concern. Martial tends to make the most of it, without piddling with pornography. The fact is that the human anatomy is one of those things, and we can manage some objectivity about it. We get nowhere by concealing the bodily fact of life and love — or we regress. The hidden evil is automatically thought of as worse, or as greater, than it is — *quod tegitur maius creditur esse malum.* So if we cannot embrace the body and enjoy its excitement and sensual pleasure we can admit the persistent power it has to generate, and to regenerate our emotional life. Martial's poems about sex insist on keeping us in touch with this rather transformable anatomy we are heirs to. He does not make a perfect score on sex, I believe; for in dealing with "transfer" or vagaries of instinct, perverse applications of sexual power, he usually ends by frowning on them or ridiculing them. His candor is not complete, his morality rests on disapproval, or sardonic humiliating laughter. But he is always ready to tangle with the mysterious forces in this labyrinth, and was lucky enough to have not one but quite a few Ariadnes to be grateful to.

Anecdotes about sexual behavior comprise only a small portion of the epigrams. The content of his work, like the contents of his books, takes many more forms. It is reality in art or in human conduct he wants us to see, and under the chemistry of his incantations it builds up its polychrome and indestructible glow like a coral reef of social events. He makes remarks, or jokes about people, praises good conduct, analyzes neurotic, advises us to heed the sensible demands of a modest hedonism. The subjects may be wanton, the poetry is always modest. There is a good deal of the Epicurean disenchantment at play, subtraction from want being a higher standard than addition to have. Martial will argue against the abuse of the mind (or picture a man with his wits in rout) and counsel either a wise forbearance or a judicious investment of the body's powers, being here very close to Juvenal's prayerful wish for a sound mind in a sound body.

Weddings, inheritances, lawsuits, vegetables, love. Revenge. Books and booksellers, other poets, doctors, rhetoricians; a few lavishly admired and long-standing friends. Innocent children abused or swept away in untimely death. Cabbages, soup, wine; patrons, togas, tunics, sandals, chair cars, carriages, barbers. Dinner parties. Dinner at home. The girls I love. The women I wonder about. My work, the people who don't like it and the people who do.

Such matters occupied Martial fully enough to provide him with the occasions for his poems and the substance of his art. He was honest enough to try and make the best of his perceptions. And so he wrote for profit, and is still read for pleasure.

The Book of the Games

1   Let Memphis
         astonished fall silent.
    The foreign wonder of the Pyramids
no longer commands our complete attention.

         Let Assyrian
      architects now refrain
      from boasting of Babylon.
  And the sensitive citizens of Ephesus
can no longer take such pride in their vast precincts of
              Artemis.

         The traffic
      of worshipful tourists
   streaming to Delos might just
as well dwindle down to nothing:

         Apollo's Altar,
      of solid pieces of horn
 interlaced, is as good as forgotten.

And Anatolians
can cease extolling
their Mausoleum for its vaulting
through empty
space.

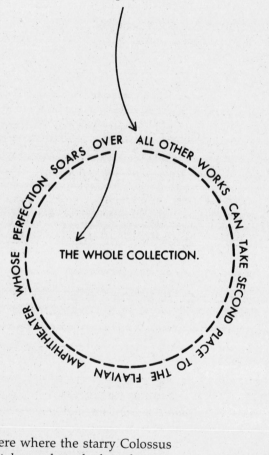

THE WHOLE COLLECTION.

(circular text) SOARS OVER ALL OTHER WORKS CAN TAKE SECOND PLACE TO THE FLAVIAN AMPHITHEATER WHOSE PERFECTION

2   Here where the starry Colossus
        takes a closer look at the stars,
    and the middle of the roadway
        is swollen with tall scaffolding,
    the hateful halls of a savage King
        once sprawled far and wide,

the One House that was a City In Itself.
  Here where we stare
open-mouthed
  at the Public Baths our generous Emperor
soon made available to us all,
  one snobbish tract of land
had evicted the poor from their homes.
  Over there, where the Portico of Claudius
unfolds its vast arcades, the palace of Nero
  kept encroaching upon the enormous distance.
So, Rome has finally
  been given back to herself.
And our Leader's princely dispensation
  allows the people of Rome the leisure to afford
pleasures once reserved
  for its Lord.

3   Is there a nation anywhere
     so outlandish
as not to furnish a spectator
    among those
in your city, Caesar?
A Rhodopeian farmer is here, from the banks
   of Orpheus' river, the Haemus,
a Sarmatian from the tribes of mares'-blood-drinkers,
an Upper Egyptian, drinking from the secret source of
  the Nile,
another whose coastline the farthest Ocean lashes;
Arabians and Sabeans have hurried here, and Cilicians
saturated in their saffron scent;
Sygambri, wearing their hair in a topknot,
Ethiopians, with their hair all in knots.
The multiple sounds of the voices of your people
are different, forming one and the same sound, calling
the father of their country
you.

4 That huge gang subversive of peace and order
 who posed a threat to the security of our citizens
 has been handed over to the people,
 and Africa's sands hardly have room for them all.
 The informer who used to send others into exile
 is himself exiled as a fugitive from the city
 Ausonia fosters. So, add this item of relief
 to the list of expenses chalked up to the account
 of our Chief of State.

5 Cheer up: Pasiphae made it with the bull:
 We saw it, in the Amphitheater.
 The hoary old story wins new credence.
 And, Caesar, old legends can stop
 admiring their own antiquity
 if what mythology sings
 the arena, for you alone, brings
 to happening again.

6 Not quite enough, oh Caesar, for Mars
 to place his invincible arms
 at your disposal, when Venus
 is seen as a fighter too,
 for your pleasure.
 The old story tells of how Hercules
 brought down the Nemean Lion
 in its massive lair. But the old story
 can fall silent when here
 in this Amphitheatrical air,
 we show women killing lions for glory.

7 Prometheus was bound to the Scythian crag
 and, tied there, fed a relentless bird
 the food of his mighty breast.

But we have seen our Number One Gangster
bare his belly to a real Calydonian Boar
and hang on the cross before our eyes.
The lacerated limbs, whose flesh and nerves
ran with blood, still quivered with life,
a part of a body that was no longer
any body;
a punishment he well deserved,
who cut a parent's throat, or a lord's, in the dead of
    night.
The crazy criminal looted our temples
of their secret gold. He set fire
to you, oh Rome, with a ferocious torch.
He outclassed all his rivals
and ancestors in the criminal class,
this fiend.
He earned a crucifixion
harsher than that depicted
in the canonical scene of fiction.

8   Daedalus, on stage, torn limb from limb
      by a Lucanian bear! How you might wish
      you had your famous wings on now!

9   That amazing rhinoceros
      parading around the arena
      in the Grand Processional—
      what combat he promised,
      what anger flared in his heart and horn,
      what a bullfight we saw in store for this bull
      who could gore a real bull like a leather ball!

10   Disloyal lion, turning on your trainer
      and mauling the hands that stroked your neck,

you paid the price for resisting the whip
when you crumpled under a shower of javelins.
And so should the manner of men conform to the style
of a Prince who is taming
our animal nature.

11   Spinning in his tracks
on the bloodstained sand
of the arena floor,
a bear was trapped in viscous lime
and his escape route cut off.
Well, why use any shiny weapons?
Keep your steel tip sheathed
and don't let the lances, brandished
in your hands, spiral on their way
to the target.
A hunter should take his prey in mid-flight
if he means to resort
to snaring bears like a bird-catching sport.

12   A savage boar hunt, presented for our pleasure
by Caesar, saw the womb of a pregnant sow
pierced with a flexible spear,
and the premature piglets
tumbled out of the breach.
Oh sharp-eyed Lucina, goddess of birth,
was that your divine conception?
The sow preferred being lacerated by spears, in order
to open the dark road of life for all her sons.
And so too, in story, Bacchus was born
by means of his mother's death,
and who can gainsay it?
A god can be born this way
and so can a beast of prey.

13   We saw the mother sow
pierced by wounding weapons.
She gave life and lost it
simultaneously.
How straight that shot was
from the balanced spear!
And I see the hand of Lucina at work in this:
For the dying animal saw both sides of Diana,
who takes the life she gives to animals.

14   The female wild boar, weighted down
with the pledge of her ripe belly, produced
her brood, being made a parent by a wound.
The litter didn't lie still, it tumbled
from the mother's womb as she fell to her death:
so resourceful Chance can draw another breath.

15   Great as your glory and fame was, Meleager,
the feats of our Prize Fighter Carpophorus
can put it in the shade. What's so great
about killing one wild Boar?
Our warrior sank his spear in a bear
charging him, the mightiest specimen
of the frozen North. And he leveled a lion
of incommensurable size, who would have brought
   honor
on Hercules' hand. Then Carpophorus stretched out
a lightning fast leopard.
And having won these prizes
Our man didn't have a scratch on him.

16   An apparatus swept off a bull
from the arena floor to heaven:

Very technical, but more godlike than *machina*.
Mythologically speaking, a bull
transported Europa across his brother's waters.
In the theater we saw a bull rising, with his rider
Hercules, to the stars. To compare
this pair of ebullient feats and their featured
players, Caesar's bull and Jove's:
They held up equally under the weight
but Caesar's rose even higher.

17   That elephant kneeling at your feet
and paying you homage, oh Caesar,
was just now a terror to a bull.
Yet he performed this act of submission
at his own volition,
not under his master's orders,
recognizing, no doubt, the god in you.

18   A tigress, the pride of the Hyrcanian Hills,
trained to lick her fearless master's hand,
ripped into a savage lion
with ravening tooth.
A nonfun phenomenon, however unique!
She never would have attempted a thing like that
while roaming her native jungles.
But after coming here to live with us
she has learned to be more ferocious.

19   This bull, just now goaded on and driven
around the whole arena, turned on the dummies
that taunted him with their leather features
and gored and tossed them to bits.

But then he fell before the horn
of a higher creation, thinking he could toss
an elephant into the air just as easily.

20   One faction shouted for Myrinus.
        Another faction proclaimed Triumphus.
        Caesar spread out both hands
        and declared both men the victors.
        A happy conclusion to the delightful dilemma,
        witty solution of our invincible Prince!

21   All the mythological paraphernalia
        offered in the landscape of Rhodope
        for the legendary tragedy of Orpheus
        has met its match in the performance
        ordered by Caesar for the arena.
        Huge rocks began to creep forward;
        the wondering trees, in a forest as fine
        as the Hesperides, started up and ran;
        every imaginable beast formed part
        of the herd, and flocks of bird
        planed over the bard's head.
        In our modern spectacle, the poet died
        at the claws of a stupid bear: In this one particular
        our *Orpheus* was *dehors d'histoire*.

22   When earth suddenly opened and disgorged
        a bear to devour Orpheus, the event was designed
        by Eurydice:
        She wanted her husband back for once and all.

23   The nervous trainer taunted his rhinoceros
       and the big brute took his time working up
       his anger: The crowd thought there might be no fight.
       But at last the ferocious temper reasserted itself
       and the big brute tossed a gigantic bear
       on his double horn, the way a bull will deflect
       the leather targets and launch them into the air.
       His aim was as sure as the steady right hand
       of our Prize Fighter Carpophorus, when he levels
       a deadly spear. With a toss of his head he hoisted
       two young bullocks together; then a buffalo
       and a bison failed to stand up against him.
       A lion, to escape the rhinoceros' charge,
       ran right into the barrage of lances.
       And now spectators, do you still complain
       of having to wait in line too long to see this?

24   As a recent arrival here from distant shores,
       watching the sacred games for the first time
       this gift of entertainment bestowed by our Emperor,
       don't be fooled by the furious naval engagement
       and waves churned up like the ocean in the arena.
       A while before, it was all good dry land
       and has only been flooded for a spectacular purpose.
       But you don't believe that? Well, watch then,
       and see that when the god of war is tired of playing
       with the waters, in a twinkling you will be blinking
       at a land engagement and saying "Hey, that was water."

25 (a) Leander didn't drown? No wonder. The water,
       furnished by our Prince, wouldn't let him go under.

   (b) Gallant Leander, courting death on his way to his love,
       tired, and nearly sank, until, we are told,

he appealed to the threatening waves, "Just let me hold
up long enough to get over there;
you can drown me on the way back."

26   The water ballet looked like Nereids
and swam through their numbers gaily.
A trident bared its teeth at us;
an anchor gave us its crooked smile;
we had the illusion of an oar, of a ship,
and the Twins, favored by sailors, presided over
the sails fluttering on the waters.
Who thought up so lifelike a show,
so like the flowing sea?
Thetis either learned it from us,
or taught it to us.

27   If earlier ages had produced a Prize Fighter
like our Carpophorus, there would have been no Wild
      Boar
terrorizing Calydon, no Fierce Bull at Marathon,
no Lion in forested Nemea. And Arcadia need not have
      trembled
at her Maenalian Boar. With Carpophorus up in arms
one death would have quenched all the Hydras,
and the total Chimaera would have completely suc-
      cumbed
to a single blow. He could have yoked
the fire-breathing Bulls without any help
from Medea and won over both of the monsters
that threatened Pasiphae. If the old story
of Hesione sacrificed to the Sea Monster
were revived, Carpophorus would set her free,
or alone effect the rescue of Andromeda.

So count up the glories of Hercules
and compare them to our Prize Fighter's record
of twenty equally fearsome beasts dispatched in a day.

28   Augustus first had the idea of staging
a battle of opposing fleets in the flooded arena
and of sounding the trumpet over the ruffled waters.
But how much greater compared to this
is the pageantry wrought by our Caesar?
Thetis and Galatea saw monsters innumerable
and unknown to them, ploughing through the waves;
Triton witnessed chariots pounding over the watery
    plain
and concluded that it was Neptune's car racing by.
Suspended over the scene like a fish out of water,
Nereus winced at setting foot in the water, as he mar-
    shaled
the battling lines of the wildly plunging ships.
Whatever is seen at the Circus or played in the Amphi-
    theater,
the water richly loaded with marvels of Caesar has
    placed
before our eyes. So let us not mention the Fucine Lake
and the pond of sinister Nero in the same breath
with this naval display of ours, a spectacle unique,
and one our descendants will still be talking about.

29   Priscus kept right on fighting
and so did Verus.
Impartial Mars
let it seesaw.
With a shout the people sought
to have it end for the heroes,

but Caesar adhered
to his policy:
Fight on, until
one man laid down his shield and raised his finger.
He did what he could
and at each new stage of the combat
gave each champion gifts
of silver pieces loaded on silver plates.
At last a solution was found
for the perfectly balanced
duel:
Each man fought well,
each one admitted defeat.
Caesar sent the symbolic sword of release
and the palm wreath of victory, to both
to register their valor and skill.
Only in your reign, oh Caesar, could it happen:
Two could fight to the end and then yield,
and both win.

30   When a doe was started by the hounds
and ran from them using all her instinctive skill
to throw them off the scent, at last she stopped
in front of the emperor's throne, and stood still there,
like one asking pardon. The hounds
held back from attacking her.
And surely such immunity was the gift of Caesar,
of his awesome presence; for his power is sacred
and makes its subjects sacrosanct:
Animals cannot lie.

31   Gaze with a kindly eye, oh Caesar,
on these paltry efforts of mine to please you.
My eager poetic behavior tumbles around
trying to find favor.

32 To yield to one greater than you
 is the mark of the kind of valor
 that accepts second place.
 But losing to one worse than you
 is some kind of real disgrace.

33 Oh Flavian line, your third issue
 has so degraded you
 it may not have been quite worth it
 to produce the former two.

Book I

To the Reader:

I hope I have shown a proper sense of restraint in my little book of poems and that no one in his right mind will take offense at them. They poke fun, of course, but they never call names; they respect the privacy of individuals, even of the lowest rank. The same cannot be said for some of our older authors, whose satirical poems named not only real persons but prominent ones. I have no wish to buy fame at that high a price and I am willing to let my own wit be the last thing to come up for consideration. I hope I can keep nasty critics from tampering with the candor of my pleasantries; and prevent them certainly from rewriting my lines. It doesn't seem quite genuine to exercise your wits over some one else's book.

As for the directness of my playful vocabulary, I do employ the saucy language of epigram. I might apologize for it except that the example of my predecessors in the genre makes such apology unnecessary. Catullus wrote in the same vein and used these familiar words, as did Marsus, Pedo, Gaetulicus, and, well, almost all poets whose works are actually read. If someone is so obsessively austere as to censor me for speaking Latin, let him read no farther than this epistle dedicatory, or for that matter let him confine his reading to the title of the book *Epigrams*. Epigrams are meant for a holiday audience, the sort who throng the theater at our Spring Festival, the Floralia. A Cato should simply not go to my theater, or if he does go he ought not to watch the performance. I can

only do justice to myself by ending this letter with a few
verses:

>   You know perfectly well the frolicsome spirit
>   of the crowd streaming into the theater
>   for the amusements of the Floralia.
>   So why did you choose to attend, oh Cato,
>   scornful and dour? You made your pointed entrance
>   only to sweep right out in disgust again.

1   Here he is, your Martial, known
     all over the world and much in demand
     for his spiky books of epigrams.
     Oh, most intelligent reader, you pay
     a compliment to a man still alive and breathing
     by granting the recognition here and now
     so rarely won by poets, and after they're dead.

2   You want my book to be with you
     wherever you go, to keep you company
     during your tiring travels? Buy a copy
     of my parchment and its nice short pages.
     Library shelves are for great long works:
     One hand can hold on to me. And in case
     you're wondering just where I am on sale,
     and wandering all over town, do let me
     lead you to my bookseller, my publisher too.
     Lucensis Secundus, that stellar freedman,
     has copies in his shop just a few doors past
     the Temple of Peace. Yes, that's his emporium
     there, as you go through the Transitorium.

3   You'd rather make a splash with the public
     and pop up in all the shops on the Argiletum
     than sink back into my comfortable shelves,

oh my little book? Think it over: you lack
experience with the fashions, tastes and distastes
of the Roman Public, the mob Mars once marshaled.
You never saw such look-down-your-Roman-noses,
such chic critics as these citizens.
Everyone's in the know, young people,
their elders: even the boys turn up their noses
like rhinoceroses.
You'll hear them shout, "How marvelous!"
as long as you're throwing them kisses
and then when they've changed their minds
you'll find yourself tossed in a blanket.
   But you don't want your author to go on
making corrections and running his reedy pen
through your happy little lines?
That confines your saucy little self, does it,
and keeps on the shelf the wings you're dying to try
on the great air outside?
All right then: Don't hide.
Escape into Rome.
But you'd be safer at home.

4   Should you be reading my books, oh Caesar,
      unwrinkle your masterly brows.
      Your conquests provide us with leisure
      to joke about them, heaven knows,
      and a leader may even take pleasure
      in supplying material for *bons mots*.
      Let an indulgent attitude seize you
      that will make you well disposed
      to the actors in naughty shows,
      and read these poems as you would watch those.
      The censor passes the risqué parts in a play
      and my pages can be very gay
      without my being that way.

5   DOMITIAN: I offer a naval engagement, and the stands
                    are crowded, and you present me with
                    epigrams.
                Do you want to go down, you and your
                    books, all hands
                overboard, Marcus Martial? Good Lord!

6   When the eagle lifted Ganymede through the air
       he took great care
       not to scar the timid burden with his claws.
       Our lions in the arena are suddenly circumspect
       with their prey: it's trained rabbits they protect,
       who jump in and out of their mouths.
       Miracle more marvelous than both—
       Can you think of any? Or of any other author?
       Each came from the highest source, the eagle
       being sent by Jove's commission,
       our tame lions at the wish of Domitian.

7   A dove is larger than a sparrow—
       I say this even in the hearing of Verona.
       My Stella's pet dove outdoes the narrow
       shape of Catullus' warbler, just as its owner
       my Stella, is a better friend than your Catullus fellow.

8   By adhering to the Stoic doctrines of a Cato
       or Thrasea, while holding on to your life
       and NOT falling on your sword, your fate, oh
       Decianus, endures the right sort of strife.
       I don't want a man who buys his fame
       at the easy price of his bloodshed.
       I want him to win acclaim
       in the present, without being dead.

9   You want to look like a pretty little fellow
        and a big shot, both. Cotta? I gotta tell you:
        A pretty little man can be pretty
        little.

10   Gemellus wants to marry Maronilla,
        ardent and generous, he keeps asking her, "Will you?"
        Is she all that pretty? You couldn't be farther off;
        what attracts him so is her ominous racking cough.

11   On special occasions each knight's ration of wine
        is ten cups, and yet, Sextilianus,
        you quaff twenty.
        How come? It's lucky you drink it straight,
        or the water reserved for the stewards would soon
        be less than plenty.

12   En route to Tivoli's cool sequestered heights,
        once honored by Hercules, at the fourth milestone from
          Rome,
        you reach the town of White Sulphur, where the steam
          curls up;
        and just beyond that lies a pretty little country villa,
        dear to the Muses and set apart in its sacred grove.
        Here, at Regulus' villa, a rough-hewn colonnaded drive
        nearly committed a most atrocious crime
        by tumbling down in ruin
        just a moment or two
        after Regulus
        had driven his chariot along its shady summer path.
        Surely, Fortune must have winced at the wrath
        we would have heaped on her unhappy head.

As it is, we can afford to laugh
at the danger Regulus
ran.
By staying up firmly in place, the columns and roof
could never have produced such effective proof
of how the gods, aloof,
watch over man.

13   His chaste wife Arria handed Paetus the sword
still wet with the blood from her side
and said, "The wound I made doesn't hurt,
but the one you make will drive me mad."

14   We have seen, oh Caesar, the pranks
and feats and nimble tricks of lions —
and the arena shows them to you, as well —
and seen a hare trapped in the playful jaws
hop out time and again and race around
this way and that, in and out of that open mouth.
How can a hungry lion bring himself to spare
an all too available hare? Oh, he's your pet, is he?
Well, no wonder, then, the lion isn't busy.

15   Most memorable of companions, Julius Martial,
perhaps our long and highly valued friendship
entitles me to say you've lived a long time:
Here you are on the eve of your sixtieth consul
and you can't count on countless days to come.
So, don't defer what might not come your way
and think of your past life as all of your life.
Oh, there's plenty of work
and the worry it's bound to cause
in store.

It's the delight that doesn't stay,
but soars away.
So, hold on to pleasure with either hand,
and put your arms around it.
It's not a wise man's part to say
"I'll live." Tomorrow's life is much too late.
Live! Today.

16   Among these lines you'll find a few
that are rather good, more that are only fair,
and a lot that are bad.
From that, Avitus, it may be deduced
just how a book is produced.

17   Titus urges me to prosecute cases.
"There's money in it"—he rehearses
this point. But there's money in wide open spaces,
Titus. The point is, I'm not a farmer.

18   How could you ruin
your good Falernian
by blending it with the dregs
of the sour stuff in Vatican kegs?
Has some bad wine done you a favor?
Have you been hurt by a good wine's flavor?
Never mind about us, your guests.
It's a sin to cut the throat of your best
Falernian, a crime to administer
poison to a pure Campanian blend.
As your friends and dinner guests, our end
is to die, no doubt.
But why take that out
on a fine and innocent wine?

19   As I remember it, Aelia, you had four teeth.
      One cough blew out two, another the third and fourth.
      So cough away happily now, all day long.
      The third cough has nothing left to let loose on.

20   What in the world possessed
      you to order mushrooms
      while every other guest
      went without? They all sat there staring.
      Caecilianus, I wish you
      a diet worthy of the riotous gullet you manifest:
      Mushrooms à la Claudius, last and best.

21   The hand that tried to kill the King
      and struck his aide instead
      condemned itself to die in the fire
      and reached out to the altar.
      The pious enemy could not endure
      such potent magic, had the hero
      hauled back from the flames,
      and ordered him set free.
      Porsenna could not bear to watch
      the hand that Scaevola had the nerve
      to hold in the coals, to fire's contempt.
      Both the glory and the story
      of that right hand grew all the greater
      for its frustrated aim:
      Had it gone straight home
      it would have gained less fame.

22   Listen, rabbit, lend me your ears! Why run
      away from the frothing mouth of yonder lion?

Its trainer hasn't taught it to render
such small game, however tender.
Those claws are kept tucked back
for using to rake the flesh of bucks.
And a lion's thirst cannot be slaked
by the two drops of blood in your veins.
Relax! It's dogs that devour hare:
You'd never fill a lion's maw,
or even tickle his paw,
come to think of it. . . .

And village boys on our frontiers in the Balkans
have nothing to fear from Caesar, come to think of it.

23 The ones you ask to dinner
are only those who bathe with you.
I wondered if by not inviting me
you were being rude, but now I see:
You just don't like me in the nude.

24 Look at the tough guy, see him Decianus?
with his hair all over the place
and the supercilious gaze
of hatred that makes his image tough
and makes you back off?
He's taken out a licence
for violence and appropriated
an unusual share of the freedom to be
he has exaggerated. Don't take stock
in his crazy shock of hair: He takes pride
in the fact that yesterday he was a bride.

25 Publish your books, Faustinus.
Think of your public!

Get the intelligent work you do off your chest.
Even Athens will like it, and our smart critics
will mention your work.
They won't overlook it.
Fame is at the door,
and you keep her waiting.
You can't bring yourself to accept
the reward of your worry?
Hurry!
Let those pages begin to live—show your face.
They will live on after you're gone in any case.

26   Sextilianus, tossing down drinks
      by the benchful, scrounging up chits
      from anywhere to cash in as yours,
      enough for five rows, or more, of Knights:
      Drink that much water, and you'd be tipsy.
      And the very best too, Vintage Opimian,
      not Paelignian stock, or Tuscan grape,
      oh no. That crock you drain so dry
      dates far back; it smacks of smoky Massic.
      If you plan to drink more than ten times your share
      you ought to order ordinary Spanish sherry.

27   Last night in my cups,
      or my brandy tumbler, at least,
      I asked you for dinner today.
      But you took me seriously, Procillus,
      and noted down carefully the words I spouted
      under the influence. A dangerous business.
      I don't like to drink with people who remember.

28   Acerra reeks of last night's wine?
      No. He drinks on into the sunshine.

29   I hear that you're reading my poems in public
     exactly as if they were yours, Fidentinus.
     If you want to pawn them off as my own
     I'll send you a copy free. But to claim
     them as yours, you ought to buy silence from me.

30   Doctor Diaulus who started as a surgeon
     has gone on to become an undertaker
     so his bedside manner is still urgent.

31   Encolpus, the darling of his centurion lord,
     has promised to cut his hair and offer it to Apollo
     when his master is promoted to Centurion First Class.
     So promote this action, Apollo,
     and let those locks fall, now
     while down does not disfigure
     his cheeks, and the tresses spill
     across his milky neck.
     Let the lad and his lord win favor from Apollo
     for some time yet by savoring their delight.
     Don't turn him into a man overnight.

32   Sabidius, I dislike you, but why this is so true
     I can't say, I can only say I don't like you.

33   When alone, Gellia never cries for the father she lost.
     If someone is with her, tears well up in her eyes,
     as if ordered to fall in. If some one looks for praise,
     he is not in mourning, Gellia.
     He truly mourns
     who mourns
     alone.

34   Lesbia, you leave the door wide open
        and the entrance unattended
        to commit your Miss demean Hers.
        You steal your pleasures right in the open.
        You're no undercover woman; in fact,
        the adulterer with you
        charms you less than someone who
        might be standing by just looking on.
        When sex is secret it vexes you.
        But even a whore will lock the door
        and draw the curtain to discourage witnesses;
        in the archways of the women who ply their trade
        beneath the walls, the vaulted rooms admit
        scarcely a sliver of light. And you might
        learn a lesson in modesty from abandoned Chione
        or jaundiced Jan, who find what cover they can
        behind the marble monuments of an old graveyard.
        Or does this censure seem to you too hard?
        I'm telling you not to be caught in the act,
        not saying you should not perform the act.

35   Cornelius, you complain that my material
        is too immaterial; not the sort a teacher
        would read with his class in school.
        But my books, like husbands, won't appeal
        to wives without some tool to govern their lives.
        You expect a hymn Hymeneal, without any mention
        of him who commands attention?
        Who sings a spring song in full dress clothes?
        Or expects mistresses to strike the pose
        of society matrons? The law hit upon
        for letting such songs go on
        their riotous way, is founded on the fact
        that they are compounded
        of sex.

If they don't make you itch
they go flat in pitch.
So lay aside your sober image
and don't carp at my games, or begrudge
us our fun. That's all we ask.
Repress your urge to cut out my works for me.
There is no worse beast than a lecher reformed
canonized as a castrated priest.

36 Affectionate brothers,
Lucan and Tullus Curvii,
to be like Castor and Pollux,
the first of you to die
should then persuade the other
to let him die for both,
saying "Brother, live your time
and then live mine." The moral:
Could any two be found in so inspired a quarrel?

37 Priding yourself on a golden chamber pot
to unload your bowels in, unlucky vessel—
you drink your wine from an ordinary glass:
So your throat is less deserving than your arse.

38 The book you read in public from
is one I wrote. But the way you moan
and mangle it turns it into your own.

39 A man to list
among rarest and best of friends
of the sort described in good old stories.

A man to list
>among the intelligent servants of Minerva,
>in both her Greek and Latin aspects,
>but who won't parade his learning.

A man to list
>as one with a sense of right and wrong,
>a regard for the good, and no sly way
>of asking special favors of the gods.

A man to list
>as possessed of energy and spirit.

Looks list a list
>of Decianus' merits.

40   Scowling over the book, you begrudge the time
>you spend on it. You envy everybody, sourpuss,
>but we don't hear of anyone envying you.

41   You want to be taken for a sophisticated wit,
>Caecilius, but you're not one bit
>amusing, you're ridiculous:

>>Like the hack who hikes across
>>from Trastevere, to hawk
>>his white sulphur matches,
>>in trade for bits of broken glass;

>>like the soupman, ladling out
>>porridge to the idle crowds;

>>like the man who owns and trains vipers;

>>like the salt-seller's slave boys;

>>like the pizza vendor shouting out
>>how hot his sausage pies are;

like a poet reciting on a street corner;

like a swivel-hipped Spanish dancer;

like a flabby-cheeked fagged-out fairy.

So how can you take yourself for smart?
Thinking you are alone a master wit
outdoing Gabba or Caballus, the old court jester.
A critic's nose is not for those
whose jokes are out of joint,
and yours don't have a point.
You don't horse around when you gag,
you nag.

42   When Portia heard of Brutus' death
and was deprived of weapons that might do her harm,
she said, "Don't you know you aren't allowed
to deny a person the right to die? My father Cato
should have impressed the lesson on you by example."
Then she swallowed a live coal
from the glowing brazier, drinking down
the sparks of death. Busybodies, that'll teach
you to keep the fatal sword so well out of reach.

43   Sixty were invited for dinner yesterday
chez Mancinus, and all we were offered
was one boar.
None of those grapes left to ripen on the vine;
none of those must-apples that taste as sweet
as a honeycomb; none of those pears, hung up
to ripen on a twig of broom plant; none of those
pomegranates the color of summer roses;
no milk-white country cheeses from Sarsina;

no olives from Picenum in tiny jars:
Bare boar, and a smallish sort, suited
to be slaughtered by an unarmed dwarf.
Even so, we weren't supposed to eat it,
just sit and look, the way we watch boars
in the Amphitheater. We reciprocate
by hoping you won't be served with boar
but served up to a boar and meet your fate.

44   If I seem to fill these pages long and short
with the frivolous rampages of lions that sport
with hares and don't devour them, and do so twice—
don't be puzzled, Stella, just be nice, and ask
me to dinner twice, and both times let the fare
be the same, good fresh hare.

45   To keep my little books from dropping dead
of brevity, I could pad with ". . . then he said."

46   When you whisper, "Hurry, I'm on the verge"
I lose the urge. Venus wanes.
Better tell me to wait. When I'm under reins
I gather speed. Then if you're panting, ready,
just say "Wait a minute. Not yet. Steady."

47   That erstwhile Doctor Diaulus
can now disembowel us.
As a licensed mortician
he's only carrying out the promise
he showed earlier as a physician.

48   Their keepers couldn't save tremendous bulls
from the crunching jaws a blithely bouncing hare
skips in and out of, a tender morsel of loot.
When the hare raced into the enemy's jaws
he raced out even faster, made more bold,
imbibing courage from a majestic source.
He's safer there than alone in the arena,
or locked up in his cage.
You clever, preposterous hare,
if you want to avoid the fangs
of hunting dogs, look somewhere
for a lion's mouth to retreat into.

49   Oh Licianus, whose famous name
is proudly hailed by Celtiberian tribes
and brings such honor to our Spanish land:
You will feast your eyes on Bilbilis,
renowned for its horses and steel,
you will see old Monte Caius, capped
with snow,
and the awesome jagged heights
of great Vadavero.
You will walk the forested paths
of fragrant Boterdus,
whose groves Pomona favors so.
You'll have a quiet swim
in the Congedus' warm stream
and those gentle lakes
where Nymphs lurk in the water.
If you're too relaxed by that,
a plunge in the scampering Salo
will tone your body up again
the way its icy waters temper steel.
And the Voberca copse, teeming with game,
will furnish you prey of your choice
within easy spearcast, while you dine.

On a cloudless summer day
you can break the grip of the heat
by a plunge in the golden Tagus,
overarched by shading trees.
Dercenna's chilling waters will slake your thirst
and Nurtha's, colder than snow.
In white-haired December when the Northwind roars
and storms rage headstrong,
you can get away to the sun-baked coasts
of Tarragona, and your own Laletania.
There you will trap and kill deer
as well as the boars bred for the purpose,
or ride down the resourceful hare;
but leave the wild stag to your gamekeeper.
And the neighboring forest will find its way
to your hospitable fireplace
surrounded by flocks of boys
who never comb their hair.
The huntsman will be invited,
and delighted, accept right away.
There won't be silver senatorial sandals
anywhere to be seen among this crowd
and nary a toga, or robes reeking of purple,
not a sign of a rich man's saucy slave,
not a client asking you for a favor,
no rich widows issuing orders!
A haggard defendant won't rout you
out of bed when you're sound asleep,
you'll stay right there all morning long.
So let some other lawyer
angle for the empty compliment,
"Splendidly argued!"
Take pity on those the world deems happy,
but humbly take to heart the genuine joy
there is in life.
Let your friend Sura have the public praise.
Sufficient fame is yours,
and life is no scoffer
in showing what she has left to offer.

50   If Aemilianus can call his cook Cut Up
       I can call mine Late For Dinner.

51   None but the noblest neck attracts majestic lions:
       So why shun those teeth, ambitious hare?
       I suppose you wish they'd lower themselves to you
         and break a neck they can't even see, not bother
       with beautiful bulls. Drop your dream of fate:
       For an enemy like that the victim should have more
         weight.

52   Quintianus, I recommend a client to you:
       My little books, if I can call them mine
       when a friend of yours recites them in public.
       If they complain of being forced into slavery,
       champion the cause and win them back their rights.
       When he says he is their lord and master, you say
       they are free, and have been manumitted by me.
       If you make this point several times, good and loud,
       the plagiarism charge will have him cowed.

53   Among the leaves you take from our book
       there lies one page of your own
       with the unmistakable stamp of authorship
       portraying you, Fidentinus, in between us:
       Like a burlap blouse on a linen dress,
       like an earthenware jug among crystal cups,
       like a black crow, flown off course and consorting
       with the swans of Leda by the waters of the Cayster—
       we can't help laughing just looking at him—
       like a stuck-up magpie, harmonizing in song
       with the dulcet and somber nightingales of Athens.

My books need not call a witness or ask for a judge
in this case, where your page
stares you in the face
inscribing THIEF
in bold relief.

54   If you have room for one more friend in your heart—
you have friends right and left—
we'd like the space, that one place.
And you ought not to turn me down
just because I'm new, and unknown
as yet as your friend.
Your old friends, Fuscus,
were originally all new friends.
So look over the new man on parade:
He might be the sort of which old friends are made.

55   Fronto, military genius, high civil servant!
Would you like to know in essence what the wishes
of your Marcus are? He wants to belong to himself;
not to have too big a field to plough. He prefers
living at unkempt ease, in quite uninvolved
circumstances. Could any one plump for marble
mosaics, cold as ice, imported from Sparta,
as surroundings in which to mutter a forced "Good
   Morning,"
when he might be endowed with the rich castoff surroundings
of the forested country, and be busy disentangling
his game-full nets in front of his own warm fireplace,
or hauling in fish that leap on his shimmering line,
or be scooping out golden honey from a plain red jar?
A plump peasant woman cook will heap his table,
that wobbles at one corner, and a charcoal oven
shirrs his eggs with fuel drawn free from the woods.

If anyone doesn't like me,
he doesn't like that life.
And I wish him well
while his skin grows pale
in the city, rife
with official strife.

56   The soaking grapes are threatened with continual rain:
     You cannot, as you wish, innkeeper, serve wine plain.

57   What sort of girl do I want,
         and not want, Flaccus?
     I don't want one too easy
         or one too hard.
     We approve of the middle ground,
         occupied by girls who neither
     fill you up or let you down.

58   That slave-dealer who asked 100,000 for a boy
     made me laugh, but Phoebus forked right over.
     My prick feels piqued, and quarrels with me,
     lavishing praise on Phoebus at my expense,
     since his has brought in Phoebus two million already
     from an anonymous rich old lady. And I might say
     that if I had as much, I'd not only pay the bounty:
     I'd raise the ante.

59   The dole I draw at Baiae is about 2.50,
     enough to starve well in those nifty surroundings.
     Give me back the gloomy baths of Lupus and Gryllus:
         Why bathe well
         when you can't eat a decent meal?

60   Go ahead, rabbit, race right into
the lion's muscular mouth, and the lion
will still think he hasn't a thing to eat.
He's trying to figure out just what back
or whose shoulders he ought to pounce on,
and how to make a deep impression on
some brave young bulls. So why fool
with the king and the lord of the jungle?
He only feeds on those he has chosen to eat.

61   Verona honors Catullus
for his scholarly poems.
Mantua is very happy with Virgil.
The hot springs at Padua
are famous because of Livy,
and Stella and Flaccus.
The fertile flooding Nile admires its Apollodorus.
The Paelignian land resounds with the name of Ovid.
Cordova eloquently claims
its one and only Lucan
and both the Senecas.

62   Cadiz, dancing for joy,
          rejoices in Canius.
       Merida wins more merit
    as my Decianus' home.
                        As for Bilbilis?
                    It may take local pride
                 in your name, Licianus.
                 And it may even murmur
                         of
                            me.

63   Linda Levine, virtuouser than the Sabines of old,
     gloomier than her own husband, and equally
       rechthaberich,
     was taking the cure at Lucrine and Avernus
     and lolling by the waters of Baiae
     when she fell right into the fire:
     Left her husband, to follow a younger man,
     ending Helen who as Penelope began.

64   It's true enough, Fabulla, you are
     a beautiful and rich young woman.
     Who could fail to see that?
     But since these praises of yourself are sung
     by you, Fabulla, you aren't rich, or beautiful, or young.

65   You said I mispronounced *figs*
     but I meant, I have piles: My seat's in a *fix*.
     I didn't say I was *eating figs*: Pain and pleasure don't
       mix.

66   You're quite mistaken, craven thief of my books,
        in thinking you acquire an actual poet's looks
          at the price of plagiarizing on plain papyrus.
             You can't win recognition for a dollar.
                Search around for esoteric songs, unfinished
                  things
                   of whose import the sole authority is he who
                     made
                       and now stands guard over the virgin pages
                         locked inside his drawer,
                           unruffled by being unrolled and rolled back up
                         with their edges scraped against the reader's
                           chin.

> A well-known book can never change its author
> but a book not yet filed down with pumice at its
>   borders
> and not yet wrapped in parchment and secured by
>   glossy knobs
> is the one to buy. And I have several. No one will
>   ever know.
> Anyone who angles for attention from the public by
>   reciting
> from another person's work should buy the author's
>   silence,
>   not his book.

67   You say I'm too free with my words, Cerylus?
Because you were not born free you're querulous.

68   Everything Rufus does refers to Naevia.
If he's happy or weeps or is silent,
if he dines or raises a toast or makes a demand
or denies a request, or complies—it all signifies
something about Naevia. If there were no Naevia
he'd have nothing to say.
                    Yesterday morning, writing
a letter of greeting to his father, he began it,
"Oh Naevia, light of my eye and light of the day,
good morning!" She read it over his shoulder
and couldn't keep a smile from stealing over her face.
But . . . Naevia is not the only one in the world,
sole judge of truth, in constant error hurled!

69   Tarentum, that liked to show its statue of Pan to us,
now makes the same fuss over Canius.

70   Go make my morning call for me, good my book,
      standing in for your master at the wealthy home
      of the Proculi. To get to the house, you pass
      Castor and Pollux, and the House of the Vestal Virgins,
      turn right and start on up the Sacred Way
      toward the impressive Palatine, with its many statues
      depicting our noble leader. Now don't dawdle, dazzled
      at the sight of the brilliant crown of rays
      that caps the Colossus blazing gloriously higher
      than the Colossus of Rhodes.

                                Keep turning with the street,
      until you meet with Bacchus in his dripping Sanctuary,
      and next past that is the temple where the Great Mother
      stands austerely beneath her hive-shaped dome
      and the painted Corybantes spin along the frieze.
      Go on; straight ahead on your left looms up
      the dazzling façade and vast atrium of a handsome
        house,
      the one you are looking for.
      Go right up to it.
      Don't be afraid they won't let you cross
      that haughty threshold—
      there isn't a doorway
      of a size like this
      that's anywhere near so accessible,
      or anywhere near so dear to Apollo and his intelligent
        sisters.
      If the host says "But why didn't Martial come along
        himself?"
      make my excuses: "You connoisseurs of good literature
      can easily judge for yourselves that paying early mor-
        ning calls
      on a patron leaves a man no time to write."

71   Let's drink six glasses to Laevia
            and seven for Justina

five for Lycas
four for Lyde
three to Ida
and let the letters in her name prescribe the round
of drinks each girl may claim.
But none of them appear—
so, Sleep, slouch over here
and listen to me say your name.

72   By reading from my works, Fidentinus,
do you think, and yearn, to be taken for a poet?
Like Aegle, fancying her pretty teeth,
when she's acquired a set of bones and Indian ivory—
like Lycoris, pleased with her white make-up
when she's blacker than a mulberry tree
that's due for collapse, weighted with fruit—
by this same line of thought—if you are called
a poet, you'll have hair when you are bald.

73   No one in town would touch your wife
so long as she was free, and willing, to boot.
But you posted guards, and suddenly brought to life
a swarm of suitors ardent after forbidden fruit
in the garden. Say, you're a wily warden.

74   He was an adulterous lover, Paula, but you
could always deny it. Then he became your husband.
So can you still say it isn't true?

75   Anyone preferring to give Linus just half
of the whole sum he wants to borrow prefers
to lose only the whole half.

76   Flaccus, native son and next new hope
of Antenor's city, Padua!
I treasure your friendship,
gained at great cost, but fully worth the effort.
Let me advise you to stop consorting
with the Nymphs and Muses.
No girl like that will give you
a single copper coin.
What do you gain from following Apollo?
It's Minerva, patron saint of lawyers,
who has her hands on all the cash,
and she knows it.
She even lends money to the gods.
What will Bacchus' ivy crown do for you?
Minerva's olive trees bend rich and black
with the clusters of fruit depending on every branch.
And except for water, Helicon
has nothing to offer but the wreaths
and lyres of the goddesses, and of course
the acclaim she bestows: "How simply marvelous!"
So, why sail to the gulf near Delphi
or pursue the naked nymphs of Thessaly,
when the Roman Forum is so much more lucrative
and so much nearer? Now, that's where you'll hear
the clink of coins, the sounding brass in the box.
The unproductive Chairs of Literature,
the lecterns in the halls where we recite,
smack only of the airy kisses
our grateful admirers fling.

77   He's awfully well, Charinus is:
                  And yet, he's pale.
Charinus doesn't drink too much:
                  And yet he's pale.
Has good digestion, Charinus has:
                  And yet he's pale.
Gets out in the sun, Charinus does:
                  And yet he's pale.

Applies cosmetics to his skin:
                    And still he's pale.
Gives girls the great linguistic rush:
Even that can't make Charinus blush.

78   When a fatal disease attacked his throat
     and spread its black contaminating force
     across his face, Festus, dry-eyed,
     consoled his weeping friends, and took his own deci-
          sion
     to accost the waters of the Stygian Lake.
     He would not distort the features of his face
     with poison, nor prolong his fate by starving.
     But exercised the choice of a cleaner stroke
     and drove his life out with a Roman death.
     Fame may well rate this death above the end
     destined for Cato. For Festus was Caesar's friend.

79   You're always doing legal work,
     you're always doing business, Attalus.
     Even if there's nothing to do,
     you're always doing something.
     If there's no case in court,
     if there's no business at hand,
     your drive takes itself out on your mules.
     At the end of your life, when there's nothing brewing,
     you'll still be busy carrying out your own undoing.

80   The night of your death you went to collect
     your unemployment insurance, Canius,
     the humiliating thing for you simply being
     that you were entitled to only the one allotment.

81   You know you're the son of a slave, Sosibianus:
        When you greet your father you always call him
            Dominus.

82

        KEEEEEEEE. . . .
                            RASH
                                    EXCLAMATION MARK
        REGULUS' COLONNADE
        JUST COLLAPSED WHOMPED
        DOWN TO AN ABSOLUTE END STOP
        A MOMENT EARLIER REG HAD DRIVEN
        HIS CHARIOT ALONG ITS BROAD EXPANSE
        THEN LONG AS HE WASNT THERE DOWN
        IT FALL BOOM DIDNT GIVE A GOOD DAMN
        LONG AS HE WASNT UNDERNEATH THE MARBLE
            STOP
        REGGO COMMA YOU MAY HAVE MADE SOME
            ENEMIES
        OVER THE YEARS BUT WHO WOULD DARE SAY
            NOW
        THE GODS ARENT IN FAVOR OF YOU QUESTION
            MARK
        THE RUIN WAS SO PERFECTLY TIMED TO AVOID
        YOUR UNDOING
                            TELLING YOU THIS GRAM IM
        YOURS AT THE SCENE OF A HARMLESS CRIME

83   Your puppy licks your face and your lips:
        No wonder, considering the way he also dips
        into turds.

84   Quirinalis doesn't want to marry,
        although he wants to have children,

and has found a way out. He screws
all his servant girls and fills
his house and estate with illegitimate knights.
As a father, therefore, he has exercised his rights.

85   A funny salesman was crying up for public auction
        some choice hillside land and some charming lots
        near the city. "Oh no, you're off," he announced,
        "If you think Marius is forced to sell. He doesn't owe
            money,
        in fact he's lending it." "So why hold this sale?" some-
            one asked.
        Then he said, "He had a run of bad luck, lost his slaves,
        his cattle, had his orchards ruined; so naturally
        he doesn't like the place." So who would bid
        on an unlucky place unless he wanted to lose his all?
        And so the stubborn land held on to its landholder.

86   Where I live I can reach out and touch
        my neighbor Novius from my window.
        Who wouldn't envy me that, and rate
        me lucky each hour of my life, so situated
        so closely associated with such a congenial friend?
        But he's as far from me as Terentianus, relegated
        to the mouth of the Blue Nile as our officer there.
        I never get to see him or listen to him, much less
        have dinner with him. In fact in the whole town
        there's no one I'm less in touch with or closer to.
        One of us ought to move farther away.
        Just rent an apartment in the same city block with him
        if you don't want to see Novius anymore,
        or rent the apartment next door.

87   To disguise your aura of last night's wines
      you gobbled down a pack of Cosmus' pastilles
      and they made your teeth nice and white—but they
          don't work
      when a mighty belch comes roaring up out of the
          depths.
      Besides, what could smell worse than this sickly blend
      of sweet, reinforced with sour contaminated breath?
      Toss away those obvious tricks, and long since discov-
          ered
      dodges. Just go on out and get good and drunk.

88   Oh my fine young lad, Alcimus, we mourn you,
      taken in the flower of youth from your master's side
      and buried in a modest grave by the side of the road.
      But let your remembering tomb be not made of marble,
      expensively wrought, and reared by the sterile sweat
      of man's hand, doomed to fall to the ground in the end.
      Accept rather this boxwood dell and these pliant vines
      that will always be fertile, and renew themselves
      with the dew of our tears. Let this green plot
      mark your place in our heart, a token of undying love.
      And when Lachesis reaches the end of the thread
      spun out for me, I want my ashes to be
      consigned to a similar mound
      based on a living ground.

89   You're always saying something in somebody's ear
      loud enough for others to overhear:
      You laugh, object, point out, you weep, you sing,
      you judge, you fall silent, you shout it
      in somebody's ear. You've got a thing about it.
      You even whisper Caesar's praises *sotto voce*
      in someone's ear—a sort of reproach, eh?

90   Never having seen you taking a man's arm, Bassa,
       realizing that no gossip attaches a lover to you,
       noticing how you were always surrounded
       by a throng of your own sex doing things for you
       and letting no man approach you, I admit I felt
       that we had another Lucretia in you.
       But you were doing the raping, Bassa,
       working out ways for identical twin genitals
       to double their fun by pretending that one—yours—
       was the man in this case, a barefaced lie
       you've conjured up a riddle only the Sphinx could solve:
       Adultery, without any man involved.

91   Although you don't publish anything, Laelius,
       you keep finding fault with my songs. So please,
       stop criticizing my stuff, or publish your own.

92   Cestos came and cried to me
       about Mamurianus fingering him.
       Mamurianus, you don't need your finger—
       take the whole guy if that's all you want,
       and need.
       You haven't got a spark of coal in your grate,
       not a coverless cot to drag out and sleep on,
       not a little old cracked cup.
       A tattered old threadbare cloak
       flaps down around your hips,
       a tiny French cape slaps at your butt.
       For meals, you inhale the steam streaming off
       from some sooty kitchen.
       You get down on all fours
       to lap water from puddles like a poodle.
       I wouldn't goose you, you're so dried out at the end.
       I might gouge your eye out, though.

So don't say I'm jealous, Mamurianus,
but go goose your guy, you economic eunuch
with your empty stomach.

93   Two soldiers and friends lie side by side,
captains both. The first to die was glad
to precede the other. And now Aquinus
lies with his brother-in-arms, Fabricius.
                The legend on the gravestone
                understates the question:
                Linked in beginnings and ends,
were there ever such steadfast friends?

94   Your singing voice was not really at its best
as long as you made love conventionally as the rest,
Aegle, old dear. Now you're in better voice,
but I wouldn't kiss you, if I had the choice.

95   You're always sounding off, always breaking in
and interrupting the lawyers, Aelius—but not for free,
oh no. You know how to cease your noise, for a fee.

96   Little scazon, my verse with the limping foot,
I hope you won't mind if I whisper some words in your
    ear
about my friend Maternus, couched in a way he alone
can take to heart. He criticizes men who sport gay
    clothes:
Crimson cloaks and scarlet mantles are for fairies,

he declares, as he dons his dark wool tunic
or thick black robes. Yet, what he does
is opposed to what he wears, and swears against.
In the baths we share he's all eyes, never looks up,
but gazes hard at the fairies' favored tools, and his lips
are busy twitching.
    So if he asks you who it is
I suspect of being like that, oh verse with the
unexpected foot, tell him I told you it was . . .
er . . . I seem to have dropped the name somewhere . . .
can't find it.

97 When everyone else is yammering away,
that's the only time you make your speeches,
and fancy yourself as a hardworking patron
pleading the case of your client.
    Well, if that's the case,
there's no one around unskilled in persuasive speaking.
Ah, but now silence reigns. Come on, Naevolus,
say a few words.

98 Diodorus is forever filing suit, toiling
in the meshes of the law. He's afflicted with gout.
But he gives nothing to the patron who tries his case
from the settlements he wins. So I see him afflicted
with arthritis that keeps his fist closed.

99 When you were hardly worth two million, Calenus,
we found you so open-handed, so generous, so stylish,
that we all wished you had ten million sesterces.
The gods listened to our private wishes and prayers,
and within the space of seven successive Kalends
four people died who left you that total amount.

You acted as if ten million had been taken from you,
not left to you. You entered a frugality phase
to the point where the one large dinner you gave in the
    year
would nick you not much more than few thin coppers,
and the seven of us, your good old former friends,
set you back the price of a set of lead spoons.
Now what shall we pray for to match that outlay
    of yours?
We wish you a hundred million sesterces, Calenus—
if that materializes, you'll starve yourself to death.

100   Afra calls many "gran'mère" and "gran'père,"
        but she's so old she's "gran," beyond compare.

101   Dead at the green young age of nineteen
        is my amanuensis Demetrius
        whose talented hand was the faithful follower
        of my words and my work, whose hand was familiar
        to Caesars.
                I did not want him to go down
        to the Stygian gloom as a slave, and to undergo
        the purgatorial fire that envelops a shackled
        sufferer, so as he lay dying I took the pains
        to renounce all my rights over him as his master.
        And I only wish that that had been good enough
                to make him well again.
        Before losing consciousness he acknowledged the re-
        ward
        and addressed me freely as patron, released as a man
        to make his own way at last to the waters of Hell.

102   The painter who did that Venus for you, Lycoris,
        was trying to get on the good side of Minerva.

103   "Now if the gods would only give me a million,"
you were saying, Scaevola, when you still couldn't claim
the sum needed to qualify as a Knight,
"Oh how I'd live in a lavish and conspicuous style!"
The gods had to laugh: and they gave you the money.
But then your toga started looking terrible,
your cloak even worse, your sandals got patched
together time and again. When you were served
ten olives at dinner, you saved out seven for later.
You used the same dishes for two meals, and you drank
those thick dark dregs we call Veientan Red.
You paid a penny for a dinner of boiled chickpeas,
you doled out a penny for a cheap bout with Venus.
We ought to sue you, you fake, unreliable trustee:
Either live a life as it ought to be,
or give that money back to the gods.

104   A leopard is fitted to the harness
          on his colorful neck.
Fearsome tigers give in patiently
          to the crack of the whip.
Wild stags champ on the golden bit.
African bears are under the control of the bridle.
A boar, mighty as one ever reared
in the forests of Calydon, obeys the tug
          of a crimson leash.
Shaggy bison are hitched up
          to wagons of war,
an elephant, attentive to his black mahout,
          glides through dance routines.
Wouldn't you say you were sitting there,
beholding a spectacle given by the gods?
But these are minor wonders, compared to seeing
lions in pursuit of small game, as the racing turns
of hares with hearts beating fast tire out the big beasts.
The lions let go of the prey, and charge off again

after it, then fondle the victim when it's caught.
And the hare is positively cozy perched in their mouths.
The lions are pleased to make a broad thoroughfare
of their jaws, and are careful, with tentative teeth,
not to puncture the delicate flesh of their tender prize.
All this, just after they've crushed young bulls to the
   ground.
Is Leo so Clement because he was trained to be?
Not at all, just aware of Caesar's Cardinal Mercy.

105   Nomentan wine, my good neighbor Ovid,
    when stored and mellowed, in the course of time
    changes its nature by grace of old age
    and sloughs off its bitter name. An old wine jar
    can wear any label it wishes.

106   You keep slipping water into your wine, Rufus.
    If a friend raises a toast you drink a drop, at the most,
    of diluted Falernian.
    Has Naevia promised to favor you
    with a marvelous night, and you're savoring
    your sober awareness, in fairness
    to the frivolous feeling in store for you?
    You sigh, fall silent, given a groan—no more for you?
    She said no? Well, heave ho, then, upend
    those cups by the score with us.
    Seize that frustrated feeling by the throat,
    and drown it by downing it. Drink deep,
    not mincingly. Don't punish yourself so convincingly.
    The night ahead was destined for sleep.

107   My dear friend Lucius Julius, you keep telling me:
    "Write something lofty. You're much too lazy."

All right, then: Give me the leisure
Maecenas gave Horace and Virgil, for pleasure
and poetry. Then I will try and fashion a work
to outlive time and rescue my name
from the ashes of oblivion.
Bulls don't like to drag their ploughs
across barren fields. Good thick soil
wears you out, but you like what it yields.

108   That's a beautiful house you have
over there in Trastevere, Gallus,
and I hope it flourishes for many more years
yet to come. My garret looks out over
the Portico of Agrippa. I'm growing old
in my little nook overlooking the Campus.
It's quite a trip for me in the morning
to get over there and say "good morning" to you,
not that it wouldn't be worth it, of course,
even if you lived much farther away.
But one toga more in the crowd of clients
thronging your threshold makes little difference,
compared to the possible one who might greet me.
So, I'll drop over around dinner time—and look—
have an early "good morning," for me, from my book.

109   That darling dog Issa—
more mischievous than Catullus' sparrow,
sweeter than a turtle dove's kisses,
more affectionate than all the gay girls,
more precious than Indian pearls—
that darling puppy Publius owns.
When she whines you'd swear she could talk,
she has a sense of joy and sorrow,
she curls up and goes to sleep on your shoulder
so still you can't hear her breathing.

She's housebroken, never makes a mess,
but puts her paw up and tugs at the covers
to get you out of bed
when she wants to go out.
So modest and chaste, she never goes catting around,
it would be hard to find a husband worthy of her.
So that death won't ravish her away totally
Publius has had her portrait painted,
a likeness so faultlessly like, that Issa herself
could not be more like. Place Issa there beside
her picture: They're either both real,
or both pictures.

110   Velox, I make my epigrams too long, you snort?
You don't write any: That's making them too short.

111   Regulus, with a reputation for goodness
equal to your wisdom, and an intellect
rivaled only by your sense of respect for the gods,
should someone wonder at the gifts
you receive, of a book and a block of incense,
he fails to see what best suits your merits.

112   Before I knew you well I called you lord
and master. Now I'm familiar with you,
my begrudging, skinflint, nonpatron, Priscus, old pal.

113   Oh yes, that collection of trifles I wrote
long ago in callow youth: I hardly recognize
the sillier items in my book of juvenilia.

If you have an hour or two to waste,
or want to ruin some good spare time,
you can ask Quintus Pollius Valernianus
for the book.
      It's thanks to him
that these insignificant things
were granted the grace of not being
just thrown
away.

114   Telesphorus Faenius owns that little park,
the well-watered plot of ground adjacent to yours,
Faustinus. There lie the ashes of his daughter,
Antulla, whose name is engraved on the stone
which should have borne his. In the natural course
of events, the father should be the first to descend
to the Stygian gloom, but since it has not transpired
in that order, may he live on and pay her the tribute
of keeping her memory green.

115   A certain girl is after me—
               I hope that makes you jealous, Procilla!
She is whiter than a spotless swan,
than silver, than snow, than lily, than privet.
But I want a certain other woman
who is blacker than night, than an ant,
than pitch, than a magpie or cricket—
            you were about to hang yourself,
            weren't you, Procilla?
But if I know you, you'll keep right on with your life.

116   Faenius has consecrated this lovely plot
of sloping ground, with its modest grove,

to the everlasting memory of one departed,
Antulla, taken all too soon from her own.
Here she lies in her tomb, and one day with her
will lie also her father and mother
should some buyer have a yearning
for this piece of land, let him banish the thought:
It will always remain in the service of its masters.

117   Each time you meet me, Lupercus, you say,
"Can't I send a boy over to pick up the book
of your epigrams? I'll send it right back
as soon as I've read them."
Don't put your slave to such trouble, Lupercus.
It's quite a way over here, at Pear Place,
and I live up three flights and they're steep.
I'll tell you where you can find what you want
much nearer. You go by the Argiletum every day,
don't you? Well, right opposite the Forum of Caesar
there's a little store, with its door plastered
with posters advertising the names of the poets.
Look for me there. You won't even have to ask
the owner, Atrectus, for me, he'll bring you
a copy from the first or second slot
nearest the counter, and there you will have
your Martial, one dollar de luxe,
smooth shaven with pumice,
decked out in a crimson cover.
"You're not worth that."
Wise
guy, Lupercus.

118   A reader who hasn't enough
with a hundred epigrams, Caedicianus,
doesn't know when he's had enough
trouble.

Go, lovely rose

Go, lovely rose
and softly wreathe
Apollinaris' hair.
And then bequeath
this honor once again
when it is white.
So, you will requite
your loving Venus' prayer.

x, 47   *The things that make life better*

The things that make life better
are these, my good friend Julius Martial:
Money you inherit and don't have to work for,
a fruitful field, an unfailing fire,
no lawsuit in sight, being seldom obliged
to don the toga, a mind unhampered by cares,
a body in good condition, and still endowed
with the strength it always had,
deliberately living on the small scale
with friends and equals, just good company;
no fussing around with costly dinner parties,
the sort of night that cheers you up
without landing you dead drunk
on a couch that's neither prudish
nor abandoned,
and then a good long sleep
that makes the darkness short.
And this above all, to accept yourself
as you really are
and to wish for nothing more.
If you live like this, my good friend Julius Martial,
you won't either long for
or wince at
your last day on earth.

*Schoolmaster! What business
have you with us*

Schoolmaster!
      What business have you with us,
   you hate-object of boys and girls?
The crested rooster has not yet shattered
the silence when we hear you rumbling
reproaches, and counting out blows with your ruler.
    The uproar in your schoolroom
    matches the sounding brass a sculptor pounds
    as he rivets the figure of a lawyer's likeness
    sitting astride the horse's back.
More noise booms from your seat of learning
than bellows from the amphitheater, when the crowd
go wild with cheering on their favorite factions.
      We therefore request that you
      let your neighbors sleep a while longer,
   not all through the night—
   it's quite all right
   to stay up a while
      and quite all wrong
      to stay up all night long.
Why not,
   just
      send your pupils home?
How much do you get for bawling out your lessons?
Would you accept the same amount to
   shut
      up?

VII, 18 *"There are thirty bad epigrams"*

"There are thirty bad epigrams
in your book, at least."
If there are that many good ones,
Lausus, I'll be pleased.

Book II

VALERIUS MARTIAL TO HIS FRIEND DECIAN, GREET-
INGS:
"What's this business with a letter?" you ask. "Don't I do
quite enough for you if I read your epigrams? What can you
say in this form that you cannot say in verse? I can see why
tragedy and comedy might need a prefatory epistle: They
can't speak in their own person. But epigrams don't need a
herald: They are quite happy to speak in their own tongue
and that a foul one. Whatever page you look at, they provide
their own explanatory epistle. So, don't do anything ridicu-
lous, please, and lead in some character twitching in his toga
for a prologue. You will find out whether it's any fun jousting
against a net-fighting gladiator with a stick. I'll be sitting in
the rows among those who shout out in protest."

By Hercules, Decian, I think you tell the truth. But what if
you knew how long and what sort of a letter you were about
to deal with: Let it be done as you say. Any readers who happen to come upon this book will owe it to you if they read
right through to the end of the first page without getting tired.

1   Oh book of mine, you could bear up
       under three hundred epigrams, but who could bear
       to read and reread you?

See what makes a short book like mine good:
First, I use less paper.
Second, my copyist will finish in an hour,
and won't waste time on my trifles.
Third, if by chance you do find a reader,
you may be as bad as you wish from one end to the
    other:
You will not lose that reader.
The dinner guest can read you through in the time
it takes to mix his drink, before the wine in his cup
warms up.
Do you feel protected by your brevity?
I hate to think of how many there will be
who still will find you all too long.

2   Crete has given us a grand name,
       Africa a greater. Victories there
       were proclaimed for Metellus Creticus
       and Scipio Africanus. Now it is Germany's turn
       to confer a glorious title on the Rhine victor:
       You, Caesar, were still a child when you earned
       the name of Caesar Germanicus.
       In the conquest of Palestine, your brother
       shared the honors with your father:
       But you won your laurels from the Hessians
       single-handed, Domitianus Germanicus.

3   . Sextus, you don't owe money. You have no debts,
       I recognize that. To be in debt, Sextus,
       a man has to have some means of paying.

4   Ammianus, how nice you are to your mother!
       How nice your mother is to you, Ammianus!

She calls you brother, you call her sister.
Why do you use these suspicious names?
Why aren't you happy just being what you are?
You think it's a manner of speaking, a joke?
Well, that's what it isn't. The mother who wishes
to be a sister doesn't enjoy
being either a mother or a sister.

5   May I lose my good health, Decian, if I don't
want to be with you all the days and nights
there are. But two miles keep us apart,
and these two make four when I walk back home.
Often you're not in. When you are, you often
won't see me. Busy, or you need some rest.
Still, to see you, two miles don't make me flinch.
But not to see you—ah, that makes me think twice
about trudging four miles.

6   Get off with it, you! Telling me to publish my books!
You hardly get to the bottom of page two, Severus,
where the knob is, when you have to start stifling
great cracking YAWNS. When I read them to you
there are some you used to snatch away from me
and copy down, and on scented love-notepaper.
You would carry some, one by one, in the fold
of your toga, to every dinner party you attended,
and every show. Yes, there are specimens like these,
and even better ones you don't know a thing about.
But what's the good of my book's being so thin
as to take up only one roll, if it takes you three days
to read through it?
I never saw a more languid lover!
You get so tired so soon on your trip
that I suppose if you drove out to Bovillae,

twelve miles from Rome, you'd have to unyoke
and spend the night at the Porta Capena.
Get off with it, you! Telling me to publish my books!

7   I mean, Atticus, you certainly can recite
beautifully!
You can plead a case in court beautifully.
And you write those beautiful histories.
You turn out beautiful poems.
You compose mimes beautifully, and your epigrams
are simply beautiful.
You sing, you dance—oh Atticus—
oh how beautifully! You are a beautiful example
of strumming on the guitar and skimming on the ball-
    field.
Of course, you don't do anything well,
but you do everything beautifully. You versatile,
great big beautiful
busybody!

8   Reader, if you find something on these pages
that's not too clear, or rather bad Latin,
it's not my mistake, it's the copyist's fault:
He was in a hurry to count out the verses for you.
If you think it was I and not he who erred,
I find you tasteless. "Still,
these are awful verses."
        As if I denied
the obvious.
They are awful. But you don't write any better.

9   I sent a note to Naevia; she didn't reply.
I suppose she won't comply.

But I think she read what I wrote
and if so, she'll be by.

10   I like those kisses you give me, Postumus,
with half your lip.
I'll let you deduct half of that half.
Would you like to give me a greater gift
of untold value?
Just keep the whole half, Postumus.

11   Because you see Selius with clouded brow, Rufus,
because he wears out his portico walking at night,
because his face is dark and silent and mournful,
because his drippy nose nearly touches the ground,
because he pounds his chest and tears his hair:
Don't think he is grieving for the death of a friend
or a brother. His wife is all right, so are his slaves,
and his pots and pans. His steward and his cook
have not cooked up anything behind his back.
What brings him grief?
He's dining at home.

12   What shall I say of the fact that your kisses
reek of myrrh, and there is no other odor
on you, ever? I sniff at the fact
that you always smell good, Postumus.
A man who always smells good
smells bad.

13   Both your judge and your lawyer, Sextus,
want their money. I advise you to pay
the money to your creditor.

Your judge will send you a bill,
your lawyer will send you a bill.
I think you should pay your creditor.

14   (Selius cruises around, hoping for an invitation to
                        dinner)
        Selius leaves nothing untried, stops at nothing
        whenever he sees that he'll have to dine at home.
        He races to the portico where the Rape of Europa
        is painted, panting out his praises for your feet,
        Paulinus, as you take your exercise there:
        Windswift feet, as fast as Achilles'.
        If Europa and environs find him no friends
        he next petitions around the Voting District,
        where people promenade past the Portico of Chiron
        and the sculpture group of Jason and the Argonauts.
        Perhaps he may find them more accommodating?
        Cheated of his hopes, he haunts the Egyptian realm
        of Isis and Serapis, with its patch of lawn
        in the Middle Temple. Isis is shaped like a cow,
        and Selius sits on his haunches before her, cowed.
        Then he is off to the Hecatonstylon
        in the Campus Martius, and then to the colonnade
        of Pompey, with its rows of trees.
        He does not shun the private baths,
        the precincts of Fortunatus,
        of Faustus, the subterranean vaults
        of Gryllus, or Lupus' Aeolian Wolf Den.
        At the public baths, Agrippine,
        Neronic, Titan, he washes time and again,
        and a third time, still in hot water.
        When he has done all this, but finds the god
        will still not will it, well-washed,
        he races back to warm Europa
        and her boxwood hedge, to see if some friend
        has turned his steps in that direction
        late in the evening.

Oh Jupiter, al fresco! You there,
the Bull, the lusty carrier,
and you, Europa, there, the girl on bullback,
won't you ask Selius to dinner?
Take him with you, I implore you.

15   Hormus, by not offering your cup
to anyone else to drink from you display real kindness,
your decent instincts. It would be sheer arrogance
to inflict your breath on another.

16   Zoilus is so ill as to have caught the fever
from his bedcovers. Suppose he were well:
What good would his crimson sheets do him,
or a mattress made in Egypt, or a pillow
dyed in Sidon's fragrant purple?
What but sickness shows such stupid wealth?
What do you have to do with doctors?
Give the medicos the gate.
If you want to recover
sleep under my cheap covers.

17   A barberess sits at the mouth of Subura Street
where the bloodstained scourges hang
and cobblers block the way to the Argiletum.
But the barberess in question doesn't shave you.
She doesn't scrape you, she rapes you.

18   Maximus, I am sorry to say
that I jump at the chance to dine at your place.

You jump at the chance to dine somewhere else.
So at least we are equals.
I trudge over early in the morning to pay my respects:
They say that you have already left to pay yours.
I am your escort: I walk before a King.
You are lord in waiting to somebody else.
So again we are equals.
It is quite enough to be a slave,
I've no desire to be the slave of a slave.
A King, Maximus, ought not to have a King.

19   Do you think, Zoilus, that I am happy at dinner?
Happy, then, Zoilus, at dinner together with you?
Any guest whom dinner with you makes happy,
Zoilus, ought to stretch out on the open road
that climbs up steeply to Castel Gandolfo.

20   Paulus buys poems, Paulus recites
his own poems. What you can buy
you are entitled to call your own.

21   To some you give kisses, Postumus —
he hissed sibilantly —
to others you give your right hand.
If you give me my choice and ask
"Which do you want?"
I much prefer your hand.

22   Apollo, what have I to do with you
and with the Nine Muses?

Behold, how the Joyful Muse harms her Bard!
Postumus used to offer me kisses
with half his lip, but now
he's beginning to plant them with both.

23   No! I refuse to identify the Postumus
of my poems. I won't, no matter how often
you ask me to. What need is there for me
to risk offending those kisses that know
how to revenge themselves?

24   If disastrous fortune makes you bankrupt,
I in my dirty clothes will cling to you,
paler than a defendant in his lawsuit.
If you are condemned to exile from your native land
I will breast the seething straits
and tear past towering crags, as your companion
in exile. Suppose fortune blesses you.
Does some of your wealth then come my way,
is there enough for two, do you give me a share?
Is your sum a big one? Candidus, surely
you're going to give me some?
For then you will be poor along with me.
But if god, with an unruffled countenance,
nods favorably in your direction, Candidus,
you will be quite alone.

25   Galla, the trouble is
you don't do what I ask you to.
But always say that you will.
If you say you will but then don't,
I ask you now: Say you won't.

26   She whistles when she breathes,
          has a hacking cough,
              gorps up spit on your chest:
     That's Naevia, all right.
     You think, do you, Bithynicus,
          you have all her property sealed and delivered?
              Well, no: That's only Naevia's way
     of turning on the charm, not turning up her heels.

27   Be sure to take Selius and his applause
     along with you when he's casting his net
     for an invitation to dinner. Have him there
     whether you're giving a reading in public,
     or trying a case in the Forum.
                    "Good show! Solid!
     What speed! Oh, that was awful of him!
     Fine! Wow! Excellent!"
     Then be sure and tell him, "Thanks.
     That's what I wanted. You've earned your dinner.
     Now SHUT UP!"

28   Go ahead and laugh, Sextillus,
         if he calls you a fairy: Let him stick out
     his middle finger. I know you're not a bugger,
     I know you're not a fucker. I know the mouth
     of hot old Lucy doesn't please you one bit.
     I admit, Sextillus, you're not any one of these.
     What are you? I don't know, but you can seize
     on the fact that there are still two possibilities.

29   Notice Rufus, wearing out the front row orchestra seats?
     Notice the rings he's wearing, sardonyx, bright even
         from here?

His cloak is soaked in Tyrian crimson dye,
his toga is made of a stuff that's whiter than snow,
his aromatic gleam hair-do pervades the theater,
his creamy bare arms hit your eyes hard,
they're so white. His brand new sandals
sport the silver crescent worn by senators only.
Scarlet leather shields his instep from bruises.
And notice those patches, artfully planted
here and there, on his forehead? Notice how neatly
they cover up the scars that date back to the time
he was first branded as a slave.

30   I asked a rich old friend of mine
        for a loan of twenty thousand:
        No trouble at all for him to give it to me,
        he was so loaded. But in answer to my request
        he said, "You know what? You want to make money?
        Become a lawyer." Look, Gaius:
        I asked you for money, not for advice.

31   I have screwed Christine a lot.
        You ask what she's got?
        Everything!

32   I'm suing Balbus, but, Ponticus, you
        don't want to tread on his toes.
        I have suit on against Licinus,
        but he is important, too. My neighbor
        Patrobas trespasses on my property.
        But you don't dare make a move
        against a man freed by Caesar.
        Laronia refuses to return my slave:
        She's hanging on to him. "Well," you say,

"She's childless, rich, old, and a widow."
I don't like appealing to a friend
who acts like a slave. I'll see
you again some day, when you're free.

33   Why don't I kiss you, Philaenis?
      You are bald.
      Why don't I kiss you, Philaenis?
      You are red.
      Why don't I kiss you, Philaenis?
      You are one-eyed.
      Anyone who kisses those parts,
      oh Philaenis, sucks.

34   Phileros means so much to you, Galla,
      that you made over your dowry to redeem him
      from slavery. Meanwhile your three sons go hungry.
      Is this the price your white-haired cunt deserves,
      an abandoned hole no proper love could fill?
      Oh mother more depraved than the Pontia
      who poisoned her sons, I trust that the gods
      will make you his mistress now and forevermore.

35   Your bowlegged shanks look like the horns
      of the crescent moon, Phoebus. I suggest
      you wash your feet in a stirrup cup.

36   Pannychus, I don't want your hair
      worn either curled or windswept.
      I don't think your skin should be
      either whiter than white or dirty.

I wouldn't want your beard to stream
like a miserable defendant's in a lawsuit
or to be done in ringlets like a Phrygian fop.
I don't like a man who is just too manly
or one who is not quite man enough.
You have hair on your chest, you bristle
with hair on your legs. But, Pannychus,
your mind is plucked.

37   Whatever is placed on the table you pack off
again, sow's breast, a haunch of pork, heath-cock,
in a serving for two; half a mullet, one whole pike,
a slice of eel, a chicken leg, wood pigeon, steeped
in its own sauce. You wrap them up in a napkin
and hand them over to your slave to carry off home.
We sit there, a mob with nothing to eat.
Don't you have any sense of my hospitality?
I asked you to dinner today, not tomorrow.

38   What return on my real estate at Nomentum?
Up there I get out of seeing you, Linus:
That's what I get out of it.

39   You shower a well-known adulteress
with crimson robes and violet gowns.
Would you like to know what gifts she most deserves?
Give her a toga, the garment worn by loose women.

40   They say Tongilius is burning up with the tertian.
But I know his wiles: He's consumed by hunger and
    thirst.

He's spreading his snares for plump thrushes,
casting his hook for mullet and for pike.
He would like some vintage wines of Opimian years,
and dark Falernian decanted in a narrow glass.
All the doctors have prescribed for Tongilius
a good cool wash. Fools, they diagnose him
as feverish on that palette. The pain is in his palate.

41   "Laugh, girl, laugh if you're sensible."
I quote the poet of Paelignus. And what Ovid?
He didn't say that to all girls;
or if he did, he still didn't say it to you,
for one reason, Maximina: You're no girl.
Of course, you still have three teeth,
three black splinters of boxwood.
If you trust your mirror and me,
you should fear breaking out in a laugh
just as much as Spanius fears the wind —
it may muss his hair — or Priscus
the touch of a hand — his robe will wrinkle —
or Fabulla, her face chalk-powdered, fears a raincloud —
it will wash her away — Sabella, well made up
with white-lead paste, fears the sun — it will melt
her down to nothing. Go get a look on your face
as stern as that of Priam's spouse, or as that
of his eldest daughter-in-law: Andromache
becomes you. Steer clear of the pantomimes
of that clever Philistion, and don't accept
invitations to amusing dinner parties,
or to any occasion that will by its saucy appeal
make your lips flap open in a good loud laugh.
You'll look better seated beside some grieving mother
who is mourning her husband or peerless brother;
you'll only be at ease in the presence of the tragic muse.
So take my advice, a variation on Ovid's:
"Weep, girl, weep, if you're sensible."

42   Why ruin the tub by washing your ass in it, Zoilus?
          To make it filthier, Zoilus, stick your head in it.

43   Ah yes, friends have all things in common,
          and these are the things you have in common,
          and keep reminding your friends of night and day,
          Candidus, in ringing tones. Your cloak,
          a Spartan import, dipped in the waters of Galaesus;
          your toga, the wool of Parma's finest flock.
          Mine is a rag the stuffed image in the arena,
          getting gored by bulls in practice, would never
          claim as his own.
                      You have cloaks from Thebes,
          processed and dyed by the descendants of Cadmus.
          My rust-red jacket would fetch about two sesterces.
          Your African lemonwood table stands on the tusks
          of Indian elephants. My beechwood board needs a piece
          of broken crockery to make its legs come level.
          Great juicy mullets on your table cover the length
          of your golden yellow platters. My boiled crab
          has the same hue as the earthenware dish it rests on.
          You have a crowd of handboys to hand you things,
          as nimble as Ganymede. What I need, my hand has to
            pass me.
          And so you have all this stuff: Yet you don't give
          a thing to an old and faithful friend; but you say,
          do you, Candidus, that friends have all things in com-
            mon?

44   I bought a slave, or perhaps a new toga;
          three or four pounds of silver plate.
          Right away Sextus the moneylender—
          you know, he's an old friend of mine—
          was afraid I might hit him for a loan.

He took care to see that I didn't by saying
out loud to himself (within my hearing):
"Let's see. . . . I owe Secundus at least seven thousand;
I owe Phoebus four, and I owe Philetus eleven. . . .
And I don't have a quarter in my strongbox."
My friend, that is what I call resourceful:
It's not easy to refuse a loan, Sextus, is it,
when you are asked for it? And even harder
to turn a man down before you have been approached.

45   Come now, Glypte: You've cut off your prick,
just because it wouldn't stand up.
You nut!
You didn't need the sword:
You were already a eunuch.

46   The meadows are painted with colorful flowers
when the bees go looting in the short-lived spring
in the mountains of Sicily.
And your clothes closets look just as colorful,
stacked with wool cloaks.
Your clothes-chest glistens with more nice robes
than anyone can count. And for your togas!
They're enough to outfit a whole tribe, in white
togas of Apulian wool selected from the finest flocks.
Your indifferent glance takes in the winter that awaits
me, your scantily clad friend, your client,
your escort whose knees rattle with the cold.
When we walk, even you feel the cold, god knows.
How much would it take, my poor fellow, for you
to give up two bolts of cloth?
You're reluctant to part with . . .
you don't want to disappoint . . .
the moths?

47   I warn you Gallus: Steer clear
       of the crafty nets of the adulteress
       I mentioned. Her body is smoother
       than the seashell cunts of Cythera's isle.
       You trust your ass with her?
       Her husband doesn't.
       He does only two things:
       Sucks, or fucks.

48   A barmaid, a butcher, a bath,
       a barber, a checker table and the pieces,
       a few books, books that I choose;
       a good friend, with some brains in his head;
       a tall slave boy who won't need to shave just yet,
       and a girl who is nice to that boy.
       Rufus, set me up with equipment like this
       in a town in the middle of nowhere like Butunti,
       and you can keep your Baths of Nero.

49   I won't marry Terry. Why?
       She's an adulteress, that's why.
       But Terry only gives it to *boys?*
       Okay, I'll marry her.

50   Lesbia, when you do it by mouth,
       and then drink water later,
       you're on the right track.
       You're applying water to the part that needs it most.

51   Hyllus, you often have but one penny left
       in your strongbox, and this one coin
       is worn down smoother than your asshole cleft.

No innkeeper, no smart baker, would deign
to take it as legal tender.
You might surrender your sovereign
to some character who takes pride in his groin.
Meanwhile, your empty stomach watches and groans
at the banquets your ass inclines
to furnish so freely. Belly whines:
"I'm hungry, you penniless pincher!"

52   Davus, the bath attendant, counts clients carefully:
     Spatale of the Enormous Tits coughs up the price of three.

53   You want freedom, Maximus?
     I don't quite believe you're asking us
     that, but if you are: Here are the formulas.
     Don't dine out,
     only buy local wine.
     Snort at nervous Cinna's gold dinner-service.
     Be happy with a toga like mine.
     Take a common girl for a mistress
     whose price won't cause you distress.
     It's all right to stoop when you go in your door.
     Screw your courage to this, you'll be free, more
     than a sheik of Iraq with a carpet for his floor.

54   Your wife's suspicions are focused on
     one part of you, and this is the proof:
     She's installed a eunuch as your custodian.
     A sharp stroke that, most unkindest reproof.

55   You want my respect, I wanted to love you,
     Sextus. I give in. Have my respect.
     But I cannot prefer someone I defer to.

56   Your wife gained a reputation in Africa, Gallus,
       for being tightfisted and grasping.
       But the stories they tell us
       are pure speculation, false. It's not her taking in,
       it's her giving out, that makes us jealous.

57   That man, casually strolling on the plaza,
       dragging along in his amethyst-tinted cloak,
       a garment dressier than Publius' impermeable
       or even the garb of Cordus, our best-dressed man
       in the great-felt-overcloak crowd—
       that man, with his mob of long-haired clients,
       all in their togas, and with his new leather litter
       and its damask curtains, waiting in the street for him—
       he just pawned his ring at Cladus' shop
       to scrape up enough dough for dinner.

58   Your new roughnapped toga makes you grin
       at mine, worn smooth. But I own the one I'm in.

59   Me called "Mica":
            Little Crumb Cake Crystal Palace;
            Domitian's Dainty Dining Room.
       From me you have a marvelous view of the Mausoleum.
       So, crowd the banquet couches, call for wine!
       Let the rose petals flutter through your fingers,
       anoint your head with gorgeous perfume!
       A god bids you remember the day of your death.

60   Hilary, my dear young fellow,
       you're sleeping with the wife of a Military Tribune,
       and only expect a mild form of punishment.

Watch it, Buster, you'll have your balls hacked off
one day, while you're at play.
"That wouldn't be legal," you say?
Is what you are doing legal today?

61   When you were young, with down on your cheeks,
your tongue made merry, midway among men.
Now, a wreck with a chopfallen face
that puts off undertakers and horrifies killers,
you dare put your mouth to a different use: Abuse!
Lashing out to revile anyone whose name pops into it.
Your venomous tongue should stick to private parts:
Then slander wouldn't make you a foulmouth.

62   Depilated! Chest, legs, arms;
and the razor leaves only fuzz
for your prick to take a stand in.
Now, Labienus, we all know
your mistress wanted it so.
But whose favor do you curry
by shearing your butt of its furry?

63   So, Milichus: One hundred thousand sesterces
was all you had left, and you blew it all
on buying Leda out of slavery on Sacred Street?
Suppose you were rich, and paid all the money you had
for love: Wouldn't that be a form of indulgence?
"Oh, I don't love her." Then it's overindulgence.

64   Laurus, you try some cases in court,
you make some well-turned public speeches,
but cannot decide what profession to follow.

In the meantime Peleus, Nestor, and Priam
will have lived their long lives, and now
it's almost too late for you to make a new start.
Take heart! Get going! Three good speakers
died this year, there's room on the rostrum.
Apply your talent, write speeches, ghost them!
The lawcourts are seething with cases fit to be tried.
Justice could keep her balance there with her eyes
    closed.
So with Virgil I say, "Once more unto the breach!"
Don't hang back. When can we expect to hear from you?
Stop wondering what you ought to be
before you don't have anything to do.

65   Saleianus, so down in the mouth?
    "It's no joke. I've just buried my wife."
    Fell stroke of fate! Grave crisis!
    You mean Secundilla, of course, the rich lady
    who brought a million to you as a dowry?
    I'm sorry it happened to you, Saleianus.

66   One ringlet went astray in the coiffure:
    Damn that disobedient hairpin!
    Lalage took revenge on the bronze mirror
    by banging it down on Plecusa's head.
    The maid swooned, smitten by the bonging
    blows, pondering those wandering tresses.
    In this distress, here's a moral, Lalage:
    Stop putting your hair in curls,
    and don't let servant girls
    touch your unbalanced head.
    Squirt salamander juice on your dome,
    or take a sharp razor to the surface.
    The poison or the blade will make your head nude
    and the mirror will reflect on your image, bare and lewd.

67   You bump into me everywhere
and keep greeting me—your voice
is the first I hear anywhere I go:
"Hey Martial, whatcha doing?"
That's your refrain whenever you see me,
ten times an hour.
Say, Postumus, whatcha doing yourself?

68   If I now call you by name when I greet you,
a man I used to hail as my king and lord,
it ought not to put me in your bad graces.
I have purchased my Liberty Cap
by selling off bundles of possessions.
A man who isn't lord of himself,
who hankers after
what kings and lords hanker after
needs a king, needs a master.
But if you cannot maintain a slave, Olus,
you can hardly afford a king, Olus.

69   Classicus, you keep saying what a dreadful bore
it is for you to accept invitations to dinner.
If you weren't lying, I'd be quite beside myself.
Apicius always liked to go out to dinner;
he was crestfallen to find himself dining at home.
If it goes against the grain to go out,
why do you go out, Classicus?
"I *have* to." True enough.
The freeloader Selius has to, too.
Ah, here comes Melior asking you out
to a proper feast, Classicus.
Now where is all your talk?
Be a man. Decline.

70   You won't let anyone wash in the tub
       before you do, Cotilus. The reason?
       You won't slosh in the waves churned up
       by some bugger before you.
       So, be the first to wash, on this condition:
       That you scrub your prick before your head.

71   You are a bright guy, Caecilianus.
       I read a few couplets of mine, and right away
       you reel off some Marsus, or quote Catullus.
       Is that comparative literature? You're showing me
       that their stuff is worse than mine?
       I think that's your motive. But still,
       I'd rather hear you read your own poems.

72   About that brawl at the party yesterday,
       Postumus—of course I don't put stock in rumors.
       But they say you took blows louder than those
       the clown hands out in the circus;
       and that Caecilius did this to you.
       At least that's the rumor that's going around.
       You say it just isn't so, and you wish I'd believe you?
       I believe you. But Caecilius has witnesses.

73   Lyris wants to know what to do:
       Tell her just to do what she does when she's sober.

74   Say, that's a crowd of toga-clad citizens
       swarming around Saufeius, so many
       I could hardly believe Regulus has so many

around him when he has won his client's acquittal
and marches home from the court, as his client
goes to give thanks in the temple.
But Maternus, don't envy Saufeius.
I hope you never have an escort like that.
The moneylenders who hold his mortgage
have ordered these flocks of friends
not to let him out of their sight.

75   A lion, used to the strokes of his confident master,
docile and tame, letting you put your hand in his mouth,
suddenly reverted to his ferocious ways
And raged worse than a beast in the mountains of
     Africa.
He snatched up two bodies, two small boys
from the group that were raking over the sand
in the bloodstained arena, to smooth it out
for the next act. He ate them with slavering tooth.
The arena has never witnessed a bloodier spectacle.
We might well protest: "You savage, treacherous pirate!
Learn a lesson from our Roman Wolf:
Save the Children!"

76   Marius left you five pounds of silver plate
in his will. But you never gave him a thing.
You didn't give him a hard time, by any chance?

77   So you find my epigrams too long, Cosconius?
You might be good at putting grease on wagon wheels.
By the same logic you no doubt find
the Colossus of Nero rather too tall
and the statue of the Boy too small.

Here's something you don't seem to know:
Masus, or Pedo, fill two pages with one epigram.
If there's nothing you'd want to take out of a poem,
the poem cannot be too long. Your couplets, though,
are superheroic.

78   Where should you keep your fish
in the warm summer days? In your warm baths,
they're colder than I would wish.

79   When you know I have guests for dinner,
you invite me to dine, Nasica.
Please accept my regrets,
I'm dining at home.

80   To escape the enemy's hands
Fannius took his own life.
Is it not mad to die
for fear of death?

81   Your palanquin, Zoilus, a portable palace, roomy!
When you loll in it, bloated, it looks rather tomby.

82   Why mutilate your slave, Ponticus,
by cutting out his tongue and hanging him on a cross?
Won't people talk about your employee's boss?

83   Oh husband, you have disfigured your wife's
       unhappy seducer; with his nose and ears your knife's
       satisfied its user. How his face misses
       its familiar features! This revenge, it meets your
       requirements? He can still ram it up their asses.

84   Remember Philoctetes, his wound and his bow?
       He killed off Paris of Troy, you know.
       Venus took revenge by turning Philoctetes
       into a notorious fairy.
       Here's a modern treatise about a very
       weird Sicilian named Sertorius, notorious
       for his habit of licking cunts. Once
       upon a time, no doubt, the stupid dunce
       did in a man who, just between us,
       must also have been most dear to Venus.

85   A flask of iced-water in a wicker holder:
       My Christmas Present to You.
       Why did I send a midsummer gift in the colder
       season? There is a reason.
       I need a toga, oh, the flimsiest kind will do.

86   I get no thrill from verse that goes backwards
       as well as forwards, though Sotades is thrilled to
           write it.
       I don't write echoing words, the way some Greeks do:
       Such verse, oh, I don't know, I just can't use it.
       I don't swoon with writhing rhythms.
       But, Classicus, will such restraint prevent
       my becoming a classical poet?

Suppose you asked a fast runner to show it
by mounting the trampoline and bouncing away?
His progress would grind to a halt. It's just as dumb
to make the writing of light verse precious hard.
As a minor Poet I see no need to be proud.
Let Ciardi read his stuff baritone aloud:
I'm hardy if gray, and I mean to stay
far from the madding crowd.

87   The girls burn with love, for Sextus they simmer
      with a face like that of an underwater swimmer.

88   You'd like to be thought of as a poet
      but refuse to recite your material?
      Be what you want, Mammercus; the public
      will tolerate you so long as you don't inflict
      your verse on public nerves.

89   I excuse you for having such fun,
      dragging out the night with much wine:
      It was Cato's vice, too, Gaurus.
      You should be praised for composing,
      despite the absence of Apollo and the Muses:
      It was Cicero's vice, and you have it.
      You throw up: And so did Mark Antony.
      You eat too much: So did Apicius.
      You like to suck others dry:
      Whose vice was that you came by?

90   Quintilian, eminent teacher
       and trainer of our unsteady youth!
       Quintilian, distinguished advocate,
       and glory of the Roman toga!
       Grant your indulgence to me,
       a poor man with years of work still in him,
       if I make an issue of living, just living.
       No one takes it seriously enough, I think.
       A man keeps putting it off: He's much too busy
       getting ahead, making more than his father
       left him, hoarding huge statues in his hall.
       He crowds the atrium with portraits of false ancestors.
       What I want is a simple home
       and a hearth that makes the ceiling sooty.
       I can afford to like that.
       I like a spring of fresh water
       and just plain grass growing around my place.
       Oh, I'll have a slave, one born in the house,
       and an unintellectual spouse.
       Sound sleep at night, and days when I never grouse.

91   Domitian, earth's glory and salvation!
       As you exist, we believe the gods exist!
       Perhaps the poems you often read
       from my hastily scribbled books
       have caught your attention: If so,
       may I be what nature could not make me,
       the "father of three children."
       I would like the rank and its perquisites.
       And if you don't like the poems, my lord,
       the title and cash would console me.
       Or have they appealed to you? To be
       a man to whom you are partial
       would make me yours truly, Martial.

92 The only person who could has granted the gift
to me of the rights of a "father of three children."
My Muses' views have their values!
So farewell, wife—I can't have you
and watch the money accrue.

93 The end of Book Two
but I hear you
asking "What happened to the First Book?"
Maybe it was ashamed to come out.
If you must have your quota,
turn this II into I
by removing a single iota.

Meno Rumore!

Why do I keep traipsing off
to my dried-out plot at Nomentum
and my untidy shack of a villa
with its sootstained household gods?
My good friend, Sparsus, a poor man
can't think in town, there's no place
left for him to have a piece of quiet.
  Early in the morning, schoolmasters
  take away your privilege of repose.
    And while it's still dark, you can hear
    the bakers out puffing their bread.
      All through the day coppersmiths
      bang away with their hammers.
        If there's a lull in business
        the money changer rattles the coins
        clattering around on his table —
        those bonging chunks of cheap metal
        minted in Nero's era.
      Go over there, you hear a
      goldsmith pounding down Spanish gold dust
      into thin leaf plates, his mallet
      flaked with bright particles of gold
      as it bounces off the worn face of his stone.
    Il y a une foule fantastique de prêtres
    qui gaze vers la déesse de guerre.

A stranded sailor starts reciting
the story of his shipwreck, begging
your sympathy, sir, and your pardon, sir,
and your contribution towards some restitution
of a semblance of decency—you see me, sir,
wrapped head to foot in these bandages,
to cover up the horrible wounds I've suffered.
Or then it's some Jew panhandling money—
a trick he learned at his mother's knee
and other low joints.

There's a steady stream of these noisemakers,
not to mention the broken-glass mender
with conjunctivitis from sulphur fumes.

Who could list the assaults
launched against good sound sleep?
For Instance:
The Exorcising of Evil Spirits

                    by Brass Gongs
   and Cymbals Clashing—

                  that's done to BREAK
The Spells
   Cast
    on
      the
        MOON—
poor Old Moon, nearly sliced right in two
by the shrieks and wails and flailing sounds
of Colchian incantations, required in that weird trade
to make their charms work right.

My good friend Sparsus, you could hardly be expected
to appreciate all these sound effects, living as you do
in the lap of luxury in that lavish town house you inherited,
your little *rus in urbe*—you won't be disturbed there!
The estate towers over our famous hills, with ample
   room
on its grounds to accommodate a metropolitan vineyard
yielding as huge a vintage as any Falernian Hill.

There's a private road for your chariot, within the limits
of your own property. Enclosed within that extent of
   ground,
you can sleep to your heart's content, and never hear
   voices
from the street, and never let light into your bedroom
unless you want it.
                         But us?
                  The laughing jostling mob
               keeps waking us up. All Rome
            seems to be standing at my bedroom door.
                       So when
                  I can't take it any more
                  and must get some sleep
                       off I creep
                       to my silly
                         villa.

VII, 85 *You've done some clever quatrains*

You've done some clever quatrains
and a couple of handsome couplets.
Compliments are in order,
but not congratulations.
It's not so hard
to turn an epigram neatly
as it is to fill a book completely.

Sulpicia's poems are read by all young girls

Sulpicia's poems are read by all young girls
who strive to please a single man
and by all new husbands
who strive to please a new-won wife.
She does not weave stories of tragic threads,
the shreds and furies of Medea or Thyestes,
she does not favor, or believe in, a Scylla
disloyal to her father, or a Byblis' incestuous love.
Sulpicia's poetry teaches honest love,
respectable, charming, diverting, pleasure.
If you rate Sulpicia's poems right
you find that none of them is slight
and none overbearingly sober.
I imagine that Egeria's pleasantries
vouchsafed to Numa, 'neath the famous cave
with its cool wet spring, were of Sulpicia's sort.
     Sappho, you would learn still more
     and be still more self-restrained
     were you Sulpicia's schoolmate, or her pupil,
     or if your pouting Phaon saw
     and admired you both together.

Admired Sulpicia, though to no avail—
since she would not consent to be
the bride of Jove Himself,
or the maiden loved by Bacchus,
or Apollo's favorite girl.
 Were her Calenus taken from her side
 she'd live alone until the day she died.

Erotion (1)

Fronto, father, and mother Flaccilla,
hold my darling Erotion firm in your memory:
Don't let her diminutive soul shiver
at the dusky shades of Hell
or flinch at the monstrous mouth
of the watchdog of Tartarus.
Had she lived six days longer,
she would have seen her sixth winter solstice.
      She was always happy,
      always at ease
      in the company of older people.
      I hope she will still, down there,
      be gaily lisping my name, in her afterlife.
Oh green earth, rest lightly on her! Do not
bear down too hard on her there, who was
never a trouble or burden to you, here.

Quite a little country place

Quite a little country place
in the city that is
you gave me, Lupus.
Rus in urbe, rather absurdly
applied to a place where one sprig of rue
makes do for the whole of Diana's grove.
A space that could huddle up under
a chattering cicada's wing,
a territory an ant could devour in a day,
that could be bounded by one rosebud leaf.
The grass it grows would total a leaf
of spikenard, or green pepper, there's not enough
room for a cucumber to stretch out straight
or a snake to fit completely into.
The garden can bear one cabbage stalk.
A gnat starves to death on the willow blossom
it gets to eat there.
                        One mole is all I need
to trench and plow my furrows.
A mushroom hasn't room to split open,
small variety figs cannot smile their welcome,
violets have no place to beckon broadly.
One mouse is enough to ravage my lands,
and the farmer fears him worse than if that *mus*
were a mighty *sus*, the Calydonian Boar variety.

A swallow can swoop down and sweep the crops off
and store the whole harvest in her nest
without even needing her claws.
You couldn't fit a half-Priapus in.
The harvest when reaped will hardly fill a snail,
and we seal our wine away in a walnut shell.
So you made some mistake, Lupus, when you prevailed
upon me to take what you rated as a good deal,
a mistake of one letter—you might have known better—
I'd much rather have had a meal.

A house on the Esquiline

A house on the Esquiline —
and one on the Aventine —
Patricius Street claims another rooftop of yours
over here you have a shrine of the widowed Great
  Mother
over there is your sacred hearth of Vesta
elsewhere you display a new bust of Jove
elsewhere a bust of Veiovis.

                Can you tell me, Maximus,
                where to meet you,
                where to find you at home?

Someone
     who
         lives
             everywhere
                  lives
Nowhere.

Juvenal

Juvenal, there you are snarled in the traffic of Rome,
poking around in the Village and its noise, or winding
your weary way up the Aventine
to pay your respects at the doorstep
of influential men, with your sweating toga
fanning you,
wearing yourself out
climbing the two spurs of the Caelian Hill—
and here am I, after many sought-after Decembers,
in my country place where Bilbilis welcomes me,
Bilbilis, known for its deposits of gold and iron.
Out here we don't dance attendance on men,
but worship nature, at her own pace,
in a pleasurable round of action, visits
to Boterdum or Platea, Celtiberian regions
with names that lie thick on the tongue.
I enjoy my night of unruffled rest
and sleep until the Third Hour, or later
and so put back in the bank all
the hundreds of hours of staying awake at night
I drew out during my thirty years in Rome.
Out here they never heard of a toga:
Your servant will toss you the nearest tunic
slung across that teetering chair over there,
when you ask for something to put on.

You are greeted by a royal fire
graced with the wood of the ilex grove nearby.
The farmer's wife has adjusted a crown of gleaming pots
along the top of the stove.
                         The gamekeeper comes in,
an attractive lad you wouldn't mind keeping some
   games
of your own with off in the woods somewhere.
    Then the smooth-shaven farm-manager
doles out their rations to the slaveboys
and orders them off to the village
to have their shoulder-length hair cut off.
Well . . . that's how we live out here
and that's how we like it,
and that will be how we die.

Book III

1   Gallia Togata, to give its Roman name
       to Provence, my provenance,
       sends you this minor item.
       When you read this book
       perhaps you will praise the preceding book:
       But then, that's my work too.
       A book born in the city that is mistress of the world
       will bring pleasure, just as a slave, born to bawl
       in a Roman household, is master of any Gaul.

2   Whose will you be, book of mine?
       Hurry now: Look for a proper patron
       so you don't get hustled right off
       to a sooty kitchen to serve as paper
       to wrap wet mackerel in, or as a cylinder cloak
       for pepper and spice. Heading straight for the arms
       of Faustinus? A clever move. You'll promenade,
       glistening with cedar oil and dressed up
       with a double title on your forehead.
       You will revel in a painted spine
       and a crimson binding will clothe you.
       Your proud table of contents will glow
       in red letters. With Faustinus to vouch for you,
       you need not fear the severest literary critic.

3   You smear your handsome face with black salve
     but refuse to wound water with your beautiful body.
     Imagine that Venus is saying in words of mine:
     "Either show your face or wash your tunic-shrouded
        body."

4   Make your way to Rome, my book. If anyone meets
     you and asks you how you got there, say by way
     of the Via Aemilia. If anyone asks where I am,
     in what place or what town, you can say I am
     at Forum Cornelii. If anyone asks why I
     have gone away, you can make a long story short
     by saying "He couldn't stand the boredom of wearing
     a striped toga." If they ask "But when will he
     come back?" you can say "He left as a poet.
     He'll come back when he can play the guitar."

5   Book of mine shall I recommend you
     to just one person or to many
     as you make your way to the city?
     If Julius Martial is the person, one
     will be enough, I assure you. His name
     is constantly on my lips. So once you get there,
     seek him out, on the Step of the First House,
     the one that Daphnis used to own, whose household
        gods
     Julius looks after now. His wife will welcome you
     and take you into her arms and hold you close,
     even though you may be dusty from your journey.
     Whichever of them you see first, him or her,
     speak up: "Marcus says hello." That will be
     quite enough. A letter of recommendation is all right
     for some unknown, but it's all wrong
     to think you have to be recommended to your own.

6   The third day after the Ides of May
     is one to be reckoned twice over
     as a festival day for you, Marcellinus.
     That day marks the first beginnings in heaven
     for your parents and marks the first sprinkling
     of your flowery cheeks for you. So praise its great gift
     of a pleasant life: It takes precedence for all fathers.

7   So that's the last of our handouts of 100 farthings,
     the money gift to the Romans a sunburnt bathman
     separates at the entrance to the baths. The allowance
     was tired of escorting citizens, anyway.
     What do you make of that, oh hunger of my friends?
     The handouts of a haughty patron have come to an end.
     "Don't look for miracles — we'll have to be given a
        salary."

8   Quintus loves Thais. Thais who? The one-eyed.
     He must be blind to want her for his bride.

9   Cinna writes poems against me? He has no readers,
     so how can they say that he's a writer?

10   Your father decided to give an allowance
     of two thousand a month and handed it over promptly
     every time on the first, even though the day after
     you ran out of funds and had to be supplied with more
     to satisfy your daily cravings. When he died
     he left you without a cent, Philomusus.
     He had used it all up disinheriting you.

11 Your girl is not one-eyed and her name is not Thais.
  So what makes you think that the couplet was aimed
  at you, Quintus? There is some slight resemblance
  between the Thais I wrote and the Lais I meant.
  But there can't be a scrap between Thais and Hermione,
  can there, Quintus? Still, you are Quintus—
  and we'll have to change the lover's name
  if Quintus balks, and let Sextus love his Thais.

12 Yesterday at dinner you offered your guests
  an unusual perfumed ointment, I admit.
  But you didn't open it, share it with them . . .
  it's piquant to smell good and have a craving for food
  but someone who smells good and then doesn't eat,
   Fabullus,
  bears, I believe, a striking resemblance to a corpse.

13 You don't want fish, you won't pluck chickens,
  you're worse than father in turning up your nose
  at boar, and then you scold and cudgel your cook
  as though he had brought in this food still raw.
  I hope I'm never as raw as that.

14 Needy Tuccius came from Spain
  to seek his fortune in Rome.
  Hearing of the Dole, he turned around
  at the Milvian Bridge, and went home.

15   Cordus has more money out at interest than anyone else
         in Rome.
      And yet he's poor? He has a consuming interest in
         Caecus.

16   Oh king of cobblers! You must be drunk: I know
      you wouldn't be doing what you are if you were sober.
      Subsidizing swordsmen in the arena is expensive.
      Those daggers drain the profits coming in from raw-
         hide.
      Oh, satrap of sandlers! You're taking it out of your own
         hide
      playing with fire, financing gladiators.
      Take my advice and stick to your last,
      if you want your money to last.

17   A steaming hot tart was brought to the table
      and passed around, too hot to handle.
      But Sabidius' throat craved it, so he puffed
      up his cheeks and blew on it three or four times,
      until it cooled off and let his fingers take it.
      It had turned to shit, so no one touched it, after all.

18   You start off telling us you have a sore throat:
      With an excuse like that you go ahead and recite?

19   The statue of a bear near the hundred columns
      of the Animal Colonnade tempted handsome young
         Hylas

to poke his gentle hand down the gaping jaws.
In the bronze unseen a poisonous viper, alone,
and fiercer than any wild beast, had made its home.
The boy didn't catch on to the trick until he felt
himself dying from the fang marks. What a pity
that bear was an imitation bear!

20   Sing, oh Muse, the activities of Canius Rufus:
Does he inscribe on immortal paper the history
of Claudius' Era, or the stories some propagandist
has concocted to whitewash Nero?
Does he compete with the sexy line of Phaedrus?
Is he wanton in lyric or serious and sage in epic?
Does he bristle in the boots of Sophocles?
Or, looking around at leisure, does he diligently browse
among sensational short stories written in Greek
for passion and pleasure, and make up his own collec-
      tion?
If that palls, does he pace the Portico of the Temple
or take a turn in the plaza of the Argonauts?
Or is he basking in the sun beneath voluptuous Europa,
and then in the late afternoon repairing to the boxwood
      hedges
to sit and keep warm away from the wind?
Is he strolling around, free at heart, with no worries?
Perhaps he's gone to bathe at the Baths of Titus,
down near the Pantheon, or is having a cold plunge
in the nude at Tigillinus' establishment.
At the welcome Fourth Hour is he with Pollio?
Is he at the gardens of Lucan or on Tullius' lawns?
He may have left for Baiae and its warm coast
and be coasting about in a boat idling on the quiet Lake
      Lucrine.
"You'd like to know what your good friend Canius is
      doing?"
He's laughing.

21   A slave who had been branded on the forehead
        saved his master from death by proscription,
        and so both men made their mark.

22   To satisfy your stomach, Apicius, you splurged
        half a million and still had left for the purge
        100,000, so with this you managed to urge
        the poison from your body and summon up the courage
        to endure hunger and thirst, and drank your medicine,
        you needy glutton. Could anything be more greedy?

23   Since you send back all the choice bits to your slaves,
        why not just take the table off its legs, too?

24   Oh Bacchus! the victim sacred to your rites
        stood before the altar, a he-goat crowned with a wreath
            of roses.
        The Etruscan priest who was sacrificing him to the god
        remarked by chance to some rough peasant standing by
        that he would cut the goat's balls with his sharp sickle
        to keep the foul smell from contaminating the dirty
            flesh.
        And as he held the animal prone on the altar of turf
        to chop the neck struggling against the knife
        the priest's big bare sack of balls revealed itself
        to the outraged congregation. So the peasant
        grabbed the priest's scrotum and slashed it off with his
            knife.
        Such was the demand of the ritual so the ancient deities
        could be duly worshipped in the medium of sacrificial
            entrails.

Well, then: You were a moment ago an Etruscan
          but are now an Egyptian priest;
          in cutting the animal's throat
          you came out the goat.

25   If you'd like to cool down your hot bath
      because Julianus will hardly dip in it,
      ask the orator Sabineius to bathe in it.
      He can freeze the hot baths of Nero.

26   You alone have estates
      You alone have cash
      You alone have gold
      You alone have crimson
      You alone have good Massic wine
      You alone have vintage Opimian
      You alone have a quick wit
      You alone have a sophisticated mind
      You alone have everything.
      Imagine trying to deny
      the obvious! You have a wife, Candidus,
      who is not yours alone,
      she's everybody's.

27   You never return my invitations
      but when I ask you to dine, you often accept.
      I wouldn't mind if you didn't invite many others.
      We each have our faults. "Now what in the world . . .?"
      Do I mean by that? Just this: I haven't the heart
      to leave you out, you haven't the decency
      to include me in, or decline.

28   Are you surprised that Marius' ear smells awful?
　　　Your fault, you're the one who whispers in it.

29   Saturn! Zoilus makes an offering to you
　　　of these his chains with the double lock.
　　　They were his rings before he earned enough
　　　to acquire the Knight's Ring.

30   The Dole has been cut off, yet you recline
　　　as a guest at dinner free of charge.
　　　Tell me, Gargilianus, what is it you do at Rome?
　　　Where did you come by that cute toga?
　　　How do you raise the rent for your musty cell?
　　　And what is the source of your dribble of cash?
　　　How come you serve as the husband of grand Chione?
　　　Justifiably, you claim to live awfully well:
　　　It's impossible to justify your existence here, though.

31   I admit that you own acres of land here and there,
　　　that your city place occupies spacious grounds,
　　　that many people in debt are enslaved to the mistress
　　　who figures as your cash account,
　　　that a solid gold surface supports your feasts.
　　　But don't snub your inferiors, Rufinus.
　　　Didymos had still more than you.
　　　Philomelus still has more.

32   "Couldn't I do it with an old woman?" Is that your
　　　　　question?
　　　Oh, I could do it even with an old woman, but you're
　　　　　not

an old woman, Matrinia, you're dead. I could do it with
   Hecuba,
I could make love to Niobe, that is, before Niobe
turned into stone, and Hecuba into a bitch.

33   I choose first the woman born free, and next
     the one who has been freed, and last the slave.
     But the slave will win first place
     if she has an independent face.

34   Chione, your name means snow, and you are, oh
     so cold, but you are also dark, and so your name
     and you are not the same.

35   Phidias embossed the inside of this bowl
     with this fish you see there.
     Pour some water in
     and watch them swim.

36   Because you prefer a recently acquired friend,
     that is, client and dependent, Fabianus,
     you insist that I improve your image
     by being the first to greet you in the morning,
     all gooseflesh, and by having your sedan chair
     drag me along as its escort through the mud,
     and by letting me trip along after you when I'm tired
     at the Tenth Hour to the Baths of Agrippa, even though
     I myself prefer to lather in the Baths of Titus.
     All this bother for thirty Decembers now
     and I'm still a raw recruit to your favor.

Have I deserved such a fate, Fabianus, I and my worn
  out
toga, with my years of service, and you still won't hand
  me
the staff of discharge?

37   You well-off people are well versed only
in cursing out your inferiors:
Un For Giving bitching is quite enriching.

38   What did you count on when you decided
to come to Rome? Did you entertain some hope
for success or progress here, Sextus? Tell me.
"I can argue a case in court more eloquently
than Cicero Himselfimus. I'd win out over
all my rivals in the Triple Forum."
But Atestinus and Civis both argued cases —
you've heard of them — and neither could earn
quite enough to pay the rent.
"Oh well, if nothing comes of that,
I will indite some great poetic work
and when you hear it you will compare
my stuff with Virgilian epic."
My dear man, that's a classical illusion:
You've seen with your own eyes the modern Ovids
and Virgils we have, every one of them shivering
in his shoddy cloak.
"Well, then, I'll haunt the houses of the rich."
They subsidize three or four at the most
and the rest of their mob of followers
are sallow-faced and pinched with hunger.
"Well what do you think I should do then?
I'm absolutely determined to live in Rome."
If you mean to be honest, you may survive
by chance.

39   One-eyed Lycoris is in love with a lad
      as handsome as Ganymede. Lycoris sees all right.

40   The silver lizard embossed by Mentor's hand on this cup
      looks so alive you hesitate to hold it.

41   Because you loaned me 100,000 from the vast sum
      bulging in your cash box, Telesinus, you appear
      to be my great friend. Actually it's I who am
      your friend, when I pay back so much more to you.

42   Applying paste to smooth out the folds in your fat belly
      only means you are rouging your belly for yourself
      instead of your lips for me. It would be more natural
      to let that minor flaw stand. The hidden evil is con-
          sidered worse.

43   It's artificial for you to look like a young man
      with your dyed hair, suddenly turning into a crow
      when just a while ago you were a swan. You won't fool
      everyone: Proserpina knows you are white-haired
      and she will make you take your mask off.

44   No one wants to meet you: When you arrive
      there's a wild rush for the exits,
      and a great vacuum develops around you.
      You want to know why?

It's because you're too much the poet.
Your art poses a decidedly dangerous threat,
it makes you more to be feared than a leaping tigress
whose cubs have been taken from her;
worse than midday heat that makes thirsty people fran-
    tic,
worse than the vengeful scorpion, are you to be feared.
Who can stand up under the punishing work
you heap on our shoulders? You read your stuff
when I'm standing still, you read your stuff
when I'm on the run, you read your stuff
when I'm on the pot. I head for the baths
where your voice bounces off the walls
and dins in my ears. I try the swimming pool—
but you won't let me swim. As I'm hurrying off
to a dinner party, you detain me to listen,
and when I get there, there you are too,
pursuing me when I'm supine on the couch,
tired, I lie down to sleep, but you
have to wake me up to listen.
Can't you bring yourself to see how much wrong
you're doing me? Here you are, a fine honest fellow,
an innocent bystander—
and we're all scared to death of you.

45 I'm not sure whether Apollo accepted
    when asked to dine with Thyestes.
    But I do know we avoid your dinners,
    Ligurinus. Gleaming napery, yes—
    and a glowing positively groaning board.
    But it loses its savor when you begin to recite.
    Better not serve me the turbot or succulent two-pound
        mullet.
    I don't want your mushrooms. I don't want your oysters.
    I just want you to clam up.

46 You expect quite a lot from me, dancing attendance
  on you in my good clothes. So I'm not coming.
  I'm sending my slave instead. He's a freedman and he
  can stand in for me. "But that's not the same thing,"
  you say. I can show you that it's a great deal more.
  I hardly have the energy to follow your litter—
  he's strong enough to carry it.
  When you get caught in a crowd he can push everybody
  out of your way with the brass knob on the pole—
  my free citizen's shoulders are weak and retiring.
  At court, when you spill out the story of your case
  I couldn't bring myself to comment at all, but he
  will roar out his "Splendidly Argued!" three times, at
   least.
  When a dispute starts up he will shout down your de-
   tractors
  in his big loud voice. But embarrassment would prevent
  my answering back those accusations in kind.
  And so you say "My client and friend, you don't do a
   thing
  for me?" Candidus, just let me perform the simple
   nameless acts
  a freedman can't perform for you.

47 Oh, Faustinus, I saw our good friend Bassus
  and his wagon loaded down with stuff
  at the Porta Capena, where the huge drops
  drip from the aqueduct and plop on the pavement.
  You know, where the street runs through the gate
  past the lovely green lawns of the Horatii estate,
  where there's the charming shrine of the baby Hercules.
  There was the cart, heaped with marvelous country
   goods;
  Big-leaf, green and white country cabbages,
  bunches of leeks, heads of dwarf lettuce,

and beets that help you reduce;
plump thrushes hanging from their hempen snares,
a hare with his neck snapped by the hunting dogs,
a suckling pig who hadn't yet eaten a bean.
Bassus wasn't sauntering on ahead of his wagon
like a Roman on a holiday, but more like the groom
he walked along with it, hugging fresh eggs
safely bedded down in straw.
Was he coming back into town? Oh no,
he was heading for the country.

48   Olus sold off his country estate and built
apartments for the poor. Now he lives in one.

49   You pour me cheap red wine while you drink Massic.
I'd rather sniff this cup than drink from it.

50   The one reason you ask us to dine with you
is to have an audience for your poetry, Ligurinus.
I slip off my sandals, and between the salad bowl
and the vinegar and fish-oil dressing, a huge book
is set. As the first course is cleared away
another book makes itself heard, then a third,
before the main course comes in.
You give us a reading from a fourth volume
and then at last a fifth. If you served
wild boar as often as this, it would go bad.
Unless you turn your poems into pieces of paper
to wrap mackerel in, you will soon
find yourself dining alone at home.

51   When I say how I like your face, Galla,
      and admire your hands and your legs
      you observe "I'm even nicer in the nude."
      But you don't go to the baths when I do.
      Are you afraid to look at me?

52   Your house cost two hundred thousand
      and a common occurrence, a fire,
      swept through it. But what was left
      brought you ten times as much.
      You're not, Tongilius, a person
      who might be guilty of arson?

53   I could do without your face,
      your neck, your hands, your legs,
      your breasts, your hips, your ass,
      your . . . well never mind the details:
      I could do without you wholly, Chloe.

54   Because I cannot give you what you want, Galla,
      it's all the easier for you to turn me down.

55   Wherever you go we think
      the make-up man has moved to town,
      as scent of cinnamon blended with woad
      is wafted on the air.
      Now, Gellia, I object to the way
      you pamper yourself with imported trifles:
      You realize
      I could make my dog smell like that
      if I wanted to.

56   I'd rather have my own well of water
than all the wines of Ravenna.
I can get a higher price for the water.

57   An innkeeper of Ravenna foxed me
by selling me straight wine
when I wanted it diluted with water.

58   Think of our friend Faustinus' villa
off in the country near Baiae, Bassus.
You won't find the walks laid out
in geometric lines past formal shrubs.
Bereft of rows of plane trees
and manicured boxwood hedges,
his place begrudges the room they take
in the broad field's spaces.
It grows wild with the savage delight
of a pure piece of land.
In age-old autumn the air is filled
with the smell of grain
floating up from the threshing floor
or loaded jars set at the corners four
of the field. In mid-November
when you feel winter closing in,
the unkempt master of the vineyard
harvests his late grapes. And from a distant valley
you hear the roars of ominous bulls. A yearling
itches for his first fight, though his horns
are barely visible knobs.
And about the place there stalks
the collective mob, a ragged army
of farm animals: a hissing goose,
jeweled peacocks, a ring-necked grouse
with burnished feathers, a bright-hued partridge,

a speckled pheasant bred in Numidia
or in unholy Colchis. A cocky rooster
treads his Rhodes Island wives.
The dovecotes echo with fluttering wings,
you hear a ringdove coo, or a turtle dove
chants low tones. A bunch of hungry pigs
snuffles up at the farm girl's apron,
and a tiny lamb is counting on its mother's milk.

      The fair-skinned household servants stand around
cheerfully enough, as the beaming hearth
lights up under a huge log, and the fire
makes the images of the gods shine on a holiday.
You won't find some pasty slug of an innkeeper
lying around the place, or a sleek gym teacher,
who wastes his oil on exercise.
Faustinus spreads his hunting nets
for greedy unsuspecting thrushes,
or reels in hooked fish with a vibrating line,
or brings home does trussed up in a heavy net.
The vegetable garden gives the city visitor a workout.
Skylarking kids are not in the least reluctant
to do what the farmer tells them to—after all,
he's not their teacher; and the mincing eunuch
enjoys the fruit of their work.

      You don't have early morning callers
coming by for no good reason, but the country man
who does show up has with him some crystal honey
still dripping in the combs, and a wheel of cheese
from the forested region of Umbria. Another farmer
merchantman has sleepy dormice to offer,
another the bleating brood of a shaggy dam,
another capons—compelled to refrain from love.
Tall maiden daughters of upright peasant farmers
offer gifts from their mothers in woven baskets.
And after work when your pleasant neighbors drop in
the table doesn't hold back food for tomorrow
but all fall to heartily, and the well-fed slave
who serves at table has never learned
to envy the guests their wine.

But Bassus, look at your house
in the fashionable suburbs
and its starved décor:
From those lofty stories you have a view
exclusively devoted to laurel trees in rows.
The Priapus holding forth in your garden
fears no marauders: There's nothing to steal.
You bring out meal from the city to feed the workman
who tends your vines, and carry to your pretty place
vegetables, eggs, chickens, fruit, cheese and wine;
you call that a country house or a misplaced town
  house?

59   A workman cobbler paid for the festivals
       in cultured Bologna, and a fuller paid for those
       in Modena. Now where will an innkeeper hold his?

60   Now that you ask me to dinner
               not, as in former times, to provide
       a meal for your client, why
               can't I share your dinner?
       You have oysters soaked in the brine of Lake Lucrine:
               I can suck out the juice
       of a mussel and nurse a cut lip;
               you get morels,
       I get pig's food, toadstools;
               for your pleasure, a mullet,
       for mine a bream. A golden-fried turtledove
               with nice fat thighs, graces your palate:
       A magpie that died in its cage, apparently,
               is set before me.
       When I have dinner with you,
       why don't I eat dinner with you?
       Since the custom is gone of your old obligation
       to feed me, we ought to share the fare.

61   Cinna, Cinna, you cynic, you say
it's nothing to ask, nothing at all.
So I suppose I'm not refusing anything, either.

62   Fact that you buy slaves for 100,000, frequently 200,000,
Fact that you quaff good wine of Old King Numa's days,
Fact that your furniture is ten times as large as you need,
Fact that your silver plate nicked you 500,000,
Fact that your gold carriage cost as much as a rural estate,
Fact that you paid more for a mule than a house would
    cost—
It all makes you feel that you have spent liberally?
Fact is: a craven spirit motivates the spendthrift.

63   "Cotilus, ah yes, there's a handsome fellow."
I hear many saying that, Cotilus, but tell me:
What is the definition of "handsome fellow"?
"One who has his curly hair neatly set,
who exudes a scent of balsam or cinnamon,
sings Egyptian songs, and whistles a Spanish air,
snakes his well-plucked arms in time to the music,
lounges at the feet of ladies in broad daylight,
prattles in someone's ear constantly,
casts his eyes over the letters he gets
and sends off an answer, who winces
when grazed by the mantle of a neighbor
standing too near, who knows just who
is in love with whom; dashes off
to dinner parties, who knows the horse Hirpinus
down to his grandsires and up to his latest descen-
    dants. . . ."
All right, so that's what it means, does it Cotilus,
that's the fellow so handsome, is it? He sounds to me
like a slippery specimen, this gorgeous guy.

64   False Ulysses is said to have sailed on past
the beguiling Sirens and the charming toll
they take of mariners, luring them to death
in excruciating joy. I can believe that.
But not even he could manage the same escape
if he heard Canius starting off on a story.

65   The fragrant breath of a lovely young girl's
bite on an apple, the scent of golden crocus,
the frosty flower that blossoms on the first grapes,
a meadow newly cropped by browsing sheep; myrtle;
an Arabian harvester; rubbed amber; the smell
of dusky frankincense aglow in the fire;
the ground lightly sprinkled by summer rain;
tresses wreathed with a crown of raisins
and perfumed with spikenard — these are the things
your kisses bring to mind, Diadumenus,
you mean, difficult boy — if only you gave
all this without the spitefulness!

66   Pompey beheaded by Ptolemy's minister,
Cicero beheaded by Antony's men — the crime
was a sacrilege for the Egyptian sword
as it was for the Roman. One of those heads
had been Rome's glory and gained her triumphs,
and rode at the head of triumphal processions,
the other had been a fountainhead of eloquence.
But Antony had less cause than did Pothinus,
who was carrying out the orders of his lord.
Antony did this evil for himself.

67   You've stopped rowing, kids,
                and you don't even realize it.
    Ho, lads, lazier than Vaternus or Rasina,
                your oars are barely dipping
    in the heavy sea, in time to the boatswain's beat.
                You call that navigating?
    It's waiting, becalmed in the noonday sun
                when Phaethon is flung
    headlong from the chariot and Aethon
                sweats in the traces
    and the midday hour yokes the tired horses
                together. You're playing in the water
    caressing the quiet waves on an unprotesting keel.
                You're not sailors at all, but cargo—
    the heroic crew of the magical Argo.

68   So far this little book has been written for you,
    good Roman matron. And if you ask for whom
    the rest of it has been written, the answer is:
    For me. We're going to the Baths now,
    the wrestling floor, the race track
    and you may withdraw: We're stripping down—
    so refrain from looking at men in the nude.
    From this point on we discard modesty.
    After the wine and roses we are no longer bashful,
    our reeling Terpsichore doesn't quite know what she's
       saying
    and comes right out with the name, no hidden allusions,
    of the thing haughty Venus parades in the sixth month,
    the Priapus that the gardener erects in the middle
    of the garden to act as its guardian, and thing
    the upright virgin looks at with horrified hand upraised.
       And so Roman matron, if I know you at all, you
      were getting
    rather tired of the book, on the point of laying it aside
    but return to it now with concern, curious to read on.

69   All the epigrams you compose are written in proper
         words:
      A prick never pops up anywhere on your pages. I ad-
         mire,
      I congratulate you: There's nothing more respectable
         than you.
      But there's hardly a form of indulgence you will find
         missing
      on any page of mine. So, sophisticated young men
      and their turned-on young women will not find as much
      to interest them here as the older man tormented by a
         mistress.
      Your words, Cosconius, holy and venerable,
      ought to be read by little boys and girls.

70   First you were the husband
      then you became the adulterous seducer
      of your former wife Aufidia. And the man
      who used to be her seducer is now her husband.
      If another man's wife
      arouses you
      though you cannot respond to your own
      can it be the security that keeps you down?

71   Since your slave's prick is as sore as your ass,
      without being a prophet I can guess what you're doing.

72   You like to fuck but you won't take a bath with me.
      I suppose it's something quite terrible: Your tits
      sag down to your stomach, or you worry
      about betraying the ridges in your vagina
      when you're naked, or exposing the scarred slot

with its huge opening, or that some inner part
may protrude from your cunt. Oh that's not it at all,
I bet. You're very beautiful naked.
But there is
a much worse fault in you:
You're so damn silly.

73   You sleep with potent young lads, Phoebus,
and what stands up for them does not stand up
for you. I wonder, Phoebus, just what to think?
I wanted to think you were effeminate
but rumor has it you are NOT a fairy.

74   You make your face smooth and bald
with depilatory salve, Gargilianus.
Have you got a thing about barbers?
And what will you do about your nails?
You can't cut them with resin solvent
and Venetian salve. If you had any sense
you'd stop betraying the poor bald place.
That treatment is usually reserved for the cunt.

75   It's been some time now since your prick
refused to rise, Lupercus, but you struggle
hard to have an erection. Colewort won't work,
salty onions, savory potherb, have no effect.
You're starting to corrupt pure cheeks
with your money, but even so enticed,
Venus will not revive. Could anyone wonder
or even believe that what won't stand up for you
would stand up if you paid a high enough price, Lupercus?

76   You perk up at old women, Bassus,
       but pout when it comes to young girls.
       The withering woman, not the pretty young thing,
       pleases you. Some frenzied whim diseases you,
       hankering after Hecuba,
       balking at Andromache.

77   Baeticus, you don't like mullet, or thrush;
       hare and boar never interest you,
       you don't like fresh cakes or squares of cornbread,
       you don't order pheasant from Colchis or Libya.
       You'd much rather wolf down capparis, and kippers
       swimming in rotted fish-oil, and pulpy rotten
       pigs' knuckles, and you chomp on frutta di mare
       and salty fried tunny fish, while lapping up
       resinated wine and turning down good Falernian.
       If you eat rotten meat, your stomach must have
       some even more secret vice.

78   Palinurus, you pissed
              over the side of the ship
     as it sailed along:
            You have to pee again?
     You're an old salt, Palinurus,
         making water again.

79   Sertorius starts up hundreds of things
       but never finishes one.
       I bet when he screws
       he doesn't persist to the end of the fun.

80   Apicius, you never find fault with a soul,
        never disparage anyone, old or young,
        yet rumor has it you wield a wicked tongue.

81   Baeticus, oh typical eunuch, what in the whorled
        is so unique for you in the female physique?
        Your tongue does business with men,
        so why did you slice off your cock
        with a jagged piece of an earthenware crock,
        to become womankind's priest?
        You were incapacitated, at least;
        but you should have been decapitated,
        pretending to castrate yourself for the Great Mother,
        all man when it comes to servicing your fellow man
        with a labial smother.

82   Whoever can be Zoilus' dinner guest
        could dine among the women who live by the Wall
        and, sober, drink to Leda in a broken jar.
        This I maintain it is to be chaste and smooth.
        He lies there flimsily clad
        on a crowded couch, and with his elbows
        he jabs his guests here and there,
        propped up on red silk cushions.
        An overripe fop stands by to fan him
        when he belches, with a fan of red feathers,
        and to hand him a toothpick.
        If he sweats, his little supine concubine
        stirs the air cool with a jade ladies' fan
        and a boy flips away flies with a myrtle wand.
        A masseuse kneads her supple fingers
        into his body, soothing the ripples
        in his muscles. As he snaps his fingers

a nimble eunuch catches the signal
and presents the pot for the golden urine
that masters the drunken penis of his saturated lord.
He dishes out wild boar sausages to the wrestlers,
sharing them with the pups licking up goose-liver
at his feet, as he rears back to toss the choice bits
over his shoulder; he confers the plump thighs
of turtledoves on his concubine.
While we are served wine from the rocky Ligures,
or wine fermented in the smoke of Marseilles,
he drinks Opimian nectar with his morons
in vessels of crystal and amber.
Well-perfumed with precious scent of Cosmus,
he shares among us on a tiny gilt shell
the hairspray a penniless adulteress
has to resort to. Now he's out, from the gulps
he's had from his giant cups. We must keep
still and listen to his snorts as we toast
each other's health by nodding our heads.
So we put up with the presumptuous honors
showered on us by this unsavory Malchion.
But we are in no position to seek revenge,
for the thing is, Rufus, he sucks.

83   Make my epigrams shorter?
      All right.
      Be
      like Chione
      to me.
      That puts it succinctly.

84   What does your compliant lady say, Gongylion?
      I don't refer to your girl, but to the young
      lass who flutters her tongue.

85   Good husband, who persuaded you
       to cut off the adulterer's nose?
       What good did that do, you fool?
       Your wife loses nothing at all
       as long as the man keeps his tool.

86   I told you ahead of time, I gave good warning
       that a modest and innocent woman like you should not
         read
       this section of my book, but there you sit holding it
       in your hand. Still, if an innocent sensible woman like
         you
       attends the performance of Latinus and Panniculus—
       that cleverly suggestive pantomiming pair—
       you might just as well read on: It's no more wicked.

87   The story goes that you have never been fucked,
       Chione, and that your midriff is inviolate. Still,
       when I see you in the Baths with your underthings on
       I keep thinking you ought to wear your brassiere
       over your eyes, and a G-string over your mouth.

88   Twin brothers, both sucking different objects—
       are they different, or identical?

89   You must eat more lettuce and mallow herbs, Phoebus:
       Your face has the set look of a constipated victim.

90   Galla wants, and doesn't want, to accommodate me,
      so I can't quite tell what she wants for herself.

91   A discharged soldier, heading home for Ravenna,
      fell in with a group of eunuch priests.
      The soldier had a young companion,
      a runaway slave who stuck right by him,
      a good-looking boy named Achillas, lithe and loose.
      The sterile men took notice and began asking
      where the boy slept, but he caught on
      to their unvoiced intentions, and told a lie—
      and they believed it. After the wine that night
      everyone trailed off to bed, but the evil group
      grabbed their swords and hacked away at an old man
      lying curled up on a corner of the couch.
      The boy watched it all from his vantage point
      in the well where he was hiding.
      In the myth of Iphigenia a deer
      was used as a substitute for the virgin girl:
      Here we have a prick standing in for a buck.

92   My wife asks me to put up with her lover, just the one.
      I feel like digging out his eyes, just the two!

93   Here you are, Miss Oldlady, having lived through
      the reigns of three hundred consuls, and you have
      three hairs left on your head, and four teeth,
      a chest like a cricket, legs the color of an ant,
      a forehead with more folds in it than a matron's gown
      and breasts that sag like spiderwebs. The mouth
      of a Nile crocodile looks narrow compared with your

gaping jaw. The croaking frogs of Ravenna prattle
more melodiously than you, and the Atrian mosquito
hums a prettier tune. You see about as well
as an owl at dawn. You smell like rank he-goats,
you have the rump and tailfeathers of a scrawny old
    duck.
And your bony cunt could outstare Diogenes,
when the lamp is out and the attendant lets you in
to join the other whores in the cemetery.
In mid-August heat the winter chill grips your bones
but fever can never gain an inch. Now, after two hun-
    dred winters,
you have the gall to want to marry, and madly seek a
    man
to cuddle up to your ashes. It's as if a piece of marble
suddenly started itching. Is someone to call you wife
and hail you as spouse whom old Philomelus recently
referred to as grandmother? I suppose you will order
your corpse dug up from the grave and stretched out
    prone
on Achoris' couch which alone might grace your wed-
    ding cry
and as a corpse-burner carry the torch for this new wed-
    ding.
Only a torch could enter that scorched cunt you own.

94   You say the rabbit's not cooked, and call for a whip.
        You'd rather beat your cook than harm a hare.

95   Naevolus, you never say "Good morning" to me first.
        You only return my greeting, if I say hello
        you will reply hello—well, even a crow
        can speak like that, and I want to know
        why you claim priority.

You're not prior, and I don't imagine
you're any better than the Martial whose greeting
you will only return. Two Caesars now
have honored me with the rights "of a father of three."
A fame I did not seek has made of me
a name on many lips and one known in many towns.
I take some pride in serving as a Roman Tribune,
and holding court where Major Waters summons you
to testify as a witness. I have had more men
made citizens by Caesar's special grant
than you have household servants in your sway.
But of course, you bugger, Naevolus; you have a way
of wagging that tail of yours nicely,
so you do have priority, I must say
you have it over me there; you win. Good Day.

96 You lick my girl but you don't screw her,
  and yet you talk as if you were the regular
  old adulterer and coxswain of the crew.
  Just let me catch you: I'll bet you
  your tongue will stop wagging.

97 I'm sending you the book, Rufus, to see
  that Chione doesn't read it. Apparently she
  has been hurt by my verse.
  She could get back at me.

98 How tight an ass should you have, Sabellus?
  The size to have a good shove with the fellows.

99 Shoemaker, you shouldn't shrink your soul
  with anger at my little book. I stick my tongue out
  at your leathery art, not at your well-buckled life.
  Let me have my harmless fun. Can't I play around
  when your profession consists of flaying around?

100 I sent off a runner
  to bring you my book, at the Sixth Hour, Rufus.
  Caught in a cloudburst,
  he arrived with it soaking wet.
  So perhaps *washing out*
  is the treatment my Third Book should get!

Pliny

Come, Comic Muse, convey my little book,
hardly learned and serious enough for him,
to eloquent Pliny. It's just a quick scramble
up the path to the Esquiline, once you've accomplished
the side-dash through the Subura. You'll see the watery
     pool
with its fountain, where sculptured Orpheus
rises over the animals clustered around him
and the eagle that stole the Trojan Boy.
Next after that you pass Albinovanus Pedo's house,
with its golden sculptured eagle, whose wingspread
is rather less than that of Jove's in the fountain.
     See that you don't burst in on Pliny at the wrong time
     in the heat of your drunken fury, pounding your foot
     against the cultivated door.
          He devotes his working day
          to uncompromising Minerva,
          preparing speeches for the ears
          of the learned lords of the civil court
          (in words that later eras will compare
          with Cicero's polished periods).
                    You'll be better off
          arriving when the lamps are lit,

your best time, when Bacchus takes command
and rose petals rule the scene, and hair
is scented and gleaming.
That's the time an unbending Cato
would even be listening,
even to me.

*My covinnus: a two-wheeled
topless British carriage*

Privacy! The terrific little two-wheeled carriage
is all mine to have and to drive
anywhere I want!
The gorgeous gift of the eloquent Aelian
to the perhaps not so deserving me.
Hey, José! Olé!
You can say anything that comes to your tongue
as you ride there along with me,
because there's no big black African
driving the horse.
And there's no little forerunner,
with his tunic tucked up,
sprinting along ahead of us,
not in this rig, there isn't.
And there's no loudmouthed coachman
anywhere in sight, and the ponies
don't talk.
If only Avitus were here to share
some secrets, I'd have no fears
of a third pair of ears.
How the day flies by,
as I
roll happily on!

Vienne

I hear,
if I can believe my ears,
that the charming provincial town
of Vienne
considers my little books
a chic possession.
I'm something of an obsession
up there among the men,
boys, young men, old.
The modest good wife reads from me
aloud, to her straitlaced husband.
I rather like being heard in Vienne—
and perhaps overheard in Lyons—
I prefer that to having my songs
echoed far out on the fringes
by people who drink at the springs
of the Nile. It's more my style
to be picked up and noticed on The Continent,
so I'd rather have that than have
my native Tagus flow with Spanish gold
for me, or draw my honey from bees imported
from high-class mountain resorts in Greece.

It looks as if I'd come,
after all,
not just to nothing.
Of course I'm not taken in by compliments
and I don't take any stock
in your disparaging words, Lausus.

Schoolmaster, take it easy!

Schoolmaster
take it easy!
Don't take it out on
your unsuspecting students!
Let that crowd of kids flock to you,
with long hair reaching to their shoulder,
and learn to love to sit and listen to you.
Let them look forward to the midday meal
they share with you.
No greater glory can crown
an arithmetic teacher
or a teacher of writing and shorthand
than a grateful circle of students.
    When the searing summer heat of mid-July
    roasts the fields blazing from the sky
    in the rays of Leo, lay aside
    that whip with the leather thongs
    and lay down your wooden ruler,
    symbols of paedagogic power.
Let the lads off, on vacation
from then until the Ides of October.
    In summer boys should be allowed to grow:
    Being healthy then is enough for them to know.

Mark Antony

Mark Antony!
You have no right to object
to Pothinus hacking down Pompey at the Pharos
when the whole list of proscribed victims you made
weighed less in the balance
than the single entry
called "Cicero's
Assassination."
How could you draw the sword across those Roman lips?
A mindless horror, which even the criminal Catiline
could not encompass, this unspeakable demented
murder.
Your killer soldier
was handsomely paid to perform
the act of hushing the voice of one man.
But of what value is the costly silence of a gifted tongue?
When all of Rome will begin to speak at length
pro Cicerone?

v, 53 *Bassus — why meditate on Medea?*

Bassus —
  why meditate on Medea?
  Why beleaguer your brain
with the barbarous banquet of Thyestes?
  And what does the theme of Niobe's tears
  actually mean to your heart,
   or Andromache's fearful story?
    Mythology has material
     more apt for your pages:
      When inspiration rages
       it would be more in order for you to invoke
images of Deucalion and Phaethon,
letting water, fire, and smoke
dominate your work.

Erotion (2)

Here lies our Erotion
        in the untimely shadow of a gravestone.
Her sixth winter hurried her on
        to an end that was destined.
I address the future owner of this land,
        and ask his yearly reverence, made
to this slender shade:
        May your household gods
forever flourish and your whole household enjoy
        a happy life—
                and may this single stone
                be the one place for grief
                on your land, alone.

Book IV

1   *Domitian's 37th birthday*
The birthday of Caesar Domitian, fairer than the light
that dawned when Jove was born in the Cretan Cave
as Mt. Ida watched from above. Long may he live!
Outlive Nestor and enjoy the untarnished glow
of days like this one. May he honor the goddess
of wisdom born by the Tritonian Lake and confer the
   prize
of a silver oak-leaf many times over again.
May he ordain the Secular Games in their majesty,
and observe the Feast of Romulus in the sunny Campus.
We ask unusual favors, oh gods of heaven,
but favors the earth deserves. Can the prayers we bran-
   dish
for so great a god, be outlandish?

2   Horatius, stunningly robed in a black cloak
was watching the games: The people, the Knights,
the Senators, our revered leader, all wore white.
A heavy snowfall suddenly came down from heaven—
and Horatius found himself wearing white.

3   Notice the thick fleece of silent snow
    floating down, to enwrap the face and chest
    of Domitian! But he is not angry at Jove,
    doesn't even shake his head, just laughs at
    the chilling flakes of frozen water.
    On his German campaigns he grew familiar
    with Arcturus, and the Northern Bear's habit
    of dousing his hair with water. But what prankster
    tosses down crystal decals from his perch
    in the heavens? Perhaps it is Caesar's son
    from his immortal throne joking with dry water,
    raining light blows on his father's head, these snows.

4   I would much rather smell like any one of these:
    A stagnant fetid swamp;
    the sulphur fumes of Albula;
    an unused aquarium; a sloppy old goat
    on top of his dam; an old, patched-over
    army boot; wool dyed twice in urine;
    the sour breath of women fasting on the Sabbath;
    the rank breath of defendants racked with sobs;
    the dying oil lamp of dirty lady Leda;
    the paste made of Sabine wine-lees;
    the murderous fumes of a cornered fox;
    a viper's nest; any one of these—
    than smell like you, Bassa.

5   A good man, a poor one, true in tongue and heart—
    what can you hope to achieve in a city like this, in Rome,
    Fabianus? You could never become
    a pimp, or a wild-parties-promoter, or the goat
    who goes around bleating at witnesses and scaring
    them into appearing in court. You couldn't seduce
    your best friend's wife, or stiffen at the call

of cold old ladies, or peddle influence on the Palatine,
or bellow out bravos for the ballet boys—and so
how will you make a living? "Well, I'm trustworthy,
a reliable friend. . . ." Tough darts, old boy,
you'll never make a name in town that way.

6   You want to appear as more innocent
than a modest virgin, and quick
to blush, when actually you're more wicked
than the type who reads erotic couplets
at Stella's poetry parties.

7   An attractive lad you were only yesterday,
and today you won't come across; so stern
just now, and just then you were so yielding;
prattling about your beard, your years, your hairs.
An unusually long long night overnight turned you
into a man and out of a boy. You jeer at me
but how in the world can this be? Is there some way
a lad yesterday can put on his manhood today?

8   The First Hour wears out us clients
calling on our patrons, and so does the Second.
The Third is reserved for gravel-voiced lawyers
arguing their cases in court.
In the Fourth Rome gets some work done.
The Fifth and the Sixth we stop for a meal
and an afternoon nap, and we round out the Seventh
with the rest of the day's appointments. The Eighth
is for oiled exercise in the palaestra, and stretches
on into the Ninth, the Ninth that summons us all to
   dinner

to crowd the cushions heaped on the couch. And then,
comes the Tenth, at last, when the way is clear for my
    books
as you, Euphemos, steward of the great Domitian,
arrange the after-dinner table, and choose for your
    master
a celestial wine of the sort he likes to unwind with,
holding the delicate cup in his mighty hand.
Then let my pleasantries find their welcome:
Our comic muse wouldn't trust itself to stroll in
on Jove early in the morning.

9   The daughter of a doctor: but you left your husband
       to throw yourself and your money at another man.
       Incroyable! You're incurable!

10   While my book is still new, hasn't shaved,
       face still wet, doesn't want to be touched—now,
       off with you, boy, lug the little gift to a dear friend,
       who has earned first right to my trifles. Sprint, but
           wait . . .
       don't forget your equipment: A pink sponge to go with
           the book,
       most apt and expedient for a gift like one of mine.
       A series of erasures could never emend
       my playful verses, Faustinus. One clean swipe can.

11   Lucius Antonius Saturninus—the name wasn't big
           enough,
       so you had yourself proclaimed Emperor by your le-
       gions on the Rhine

and staged a mutiny under the Northern Bear, a rebel-
lion
as arrogant as his who wore the colors of a Pharaoh's
wife.
But Antony foundered off the promontory of Actium,
and
have you forgotten how heavily an angry fate swamped
him
in waves of retribution? Did the Rhine offer you some
larger
opportunity than your namesake's, was there more
room up there
in those northern waters? Antonius the First was de-
feated
by our Roman weapons, and traitor though he was,
he was an Emperor in name, quite unlike you.

12   Thais, you don't say No to anyone; and you aren't
embarrassed.
But you don't say No to *anything* either: And still feel
unharassed?

13   Hail to the wedding of Claudia Peregrina and my good
friend Pudens!
Oh, Spirit of Marriage, bless the rite with your blazing
torch!
We don't often find the best cinnamon allied with its
companion nard,
or fine Massic wine with Athenian honey. Nor can the
vines
be better wedded to the elms, the lotus more compan-
ionable
to the water, the myrtle to the stream it loves.

And so may clear understanding
and gracious agreement
ever dwell at their nuptial couch.
May she love him when he grows old
and seem in her husband's eyes as she does today
a young bride who never grows old.

14   Oh epic master, Silius Italicus,
honor and pride of the sisters
who guard the Castalian Springs,
engaged as you are in your long account
of the ferocious treachery, and the wiles,
of Hannibal, as in verse you turn the flanks
of the light-armed Carthaginian troops
and make them yield to the Scipios,
discard your somber mien a while.
It's the casual month of December, and the dice with a
    tempting sound
rattle around in their boxes, the knucklebones are clat-
    tering,
a game of tropa is on, and we're watching that single
    chip.
So, unbend a little and be at ease among our Muses,
the local Italian girls. Smooth out those wrinkles in your
    brow;
cast an eye over my books, still wet with frivolous say-
    ings.
Catullus once dared address mighty Virgil this way
and sent his Song of the Sparrow to the Master of Arms
    and Men.

15   Yesterday at dawn you asked me for a loan of a thousand
for six or seven days. "I just don't have it,"
I told you, Caecilianus. Now you say you need a few
    things

for a small dinner party for a friend who's due in town,
some plates and a silver serving dish. Are you just
   stupid,
or do you just think I am, my friend? I told you No
to a thousand. So now I'll fork over five?

16   So long as she was your father's wife, they said
you weren't the stepson of your stepmother.
But of course it couldn't be proved, Gallus, so long
as your father was still alive. Now that he isn't,
you have your stepmother at home. Well, get Cicero
up out of the underworld and let him defend you,
or let Regulus take the case, you won't be acquitted.
A stepmother who goes right on being a stepmother
after the father's death, never was one at all.

17   You want me to write some lines against Lycisca
that will make her turn red and get mad. Tsk, tsk, ah
there . . . just so she can be had . . . by you?

18   Down by the gate near the Pantheon
where the stones are slippery with the steady rain,
an icicle worked loose and severed the throat
of a boy walking by underneath the slick roofs.
And having accomplished its cruel mission,
the slender sword-tip melted in the warm wound.
Is anything denied the fiendish whims of Fortune?
Is death not everywhere, if water can cut our throats?

19   Je vous envoie ce pullover-ci,
       woven by a French woman near the Seine—
       an *endromis*, to give it the Spartan name.
       Not an imaginative gift, a French sweater,
       but not one to be shrugged off, either, this cold
          December,
       when you've had a good game of catch and are glowing
       warm and shining with liniment, or after a hot
       and dusty session of handball, or after a bout
       with the punching bag, or after trying to outsprint
       slender Athos in the final heat. Then this new pullover
       will keep the clenching cold from weaving its way
       into your sweating pores. Or it will keep you dry
       if cloudy Iris pounces down in a cloudburst. And so,
       covered by a gift like this, you'll laugh at the winds
       and the rain, safer than if attired
       in a linen cloak from Tyre.

20   Caerellia says she's too old: She's just a child.
       Gallia says she's so young: She's an old hag.
       They're both unbearable: One's too silly, one's too chilly.

21   Sergius swears by the hollow sky that there are no gods,
       and the truth is plain, since he,
       denouncing them, is wealthy as can be.

22   Cleopatra not only passed the test
       of the wedding night, but was still so alluring
       to her husband that she had to dive into the gleaming
       swimming pool to evade his clutches. But the water
       gave her away by glistening where she lay submerged.

So, the lilies beneath a pane of glass
can be seen and counted, and so the rose,
ensconced in crystal, lies disclosed.
I dove, and plunging in snatched kisses
as she tried to fight me off.
The transparent water—too obvious—kept me at bay.
Kisses were all I managed to get that way.

23   Thalia, dear Comic Muse, forever judging,
analyzing, wondering who your favorite poet
is, and who is second best, and who
ranks highest in comparison with the Greek epigram—
while you hesitate, dear Comic Muse, Callimachus
has taken off his crown and passed it on
to the graceful and expressive Brutianus.
But when this poet has done with Athenian wit
and finished his doting dalliance with Minerva
and the Roman mind, I only ask to be thought of
as the next candidate for Thalia's funny favors.

24   Lycoris has seen all of her friends out of life:
I can only hope that she makes a friend of my wife.

25   The shores of Altinum rival the residences
of the fashionably great at Baiae.
The forest where Phaethon found his funeral pyre,
and where Sola, loveliest of the Dryads, married Faunus
wedded to the son of Antenor
beside the Euganean Lake.
There too we see you, Aquileia,
graced by the river Timavus, and Leda's sons,

where Cyllarus, Pollux' steed, drank from sevenfold
   waters.
For me not seaside Baiae, but distant Altinum
will be a quiet retreat in later years when I retire
if I earn the leisure I'm writing to acquire.

26   Would you like to know how much I've lost
by not paying you the early morning call
for one whole year? Postumus, this is what
has been lost to us: 300 sesterces, twice;
200 sesterces—I missed that three times.
Do excuse me: The economy toga I'm wearing
costs much more than that.

27   Augustus, you have the habit of praising
my little books. An envious critic says
you shouldn't, but still you don't desist.
And why have you given gifts no other person
could grant me, lavishing them on something
praised elsewhere by more than one voice?
The result is that envious criticism
is again busy gnawing its nails. So, give
her still more reason to suffer, I pray you, Caesar.

28   Chloe, you've showered your nice young man,
Lupercus, with: Spanish capes and Tyrian cloaks
of crimson and scarlet, and a white wool toga
that was washed in the warm Galaesus, and gems,
Indian sardonyx and emeralds from Scythia, and
a hundred pieces of gold newly minted; whatever
he wants you give him and then some. You poor little
thing, peeled for the love of a slave. He'll have
you stripped down to a totally bare figure.

29   The thing that bothers me most
       about these epigrams is:
       There are too many of them.
       You know, Pudens, how we appreciate
       the uncommonplace: The first of the fruit,
       Roses in winter, are what we value.
       Contempt makes a spiteful mistress
       desirable; an open door does not
       keep a young man on the string.
       Persius is reckoned with more often,
       in his one little book of Satires, than Marsus,
       in his lengthy and breathless epic.
       So pick a single book of mine,
       say to yourself, that's all he wrote:
       It may become one of note.

30   No fishing! Angler, keep your distance
       from Domitian's private pool at Baiae
       adjoining the Lucrine Lake, where the waters swim
       with sacred fish your hook would desecrate.
       They know their lord and nibble from his hand,
       the noble palm that holds the world in hand.
       He has named them all; they dart up when he calls them.
       How do you like that!
       One day a dumb Libyan was hauling
       a prize up out of these depths with his quivering rod
       when suddenly he lost his sight, and couldn't see
       the fish he caught. So today he sits there and begs,
       beside the waters of Baiae, cursing the hooks
       he trespassed with. So angler, while you can,
       step back without infringing, and toss them food,
       not bait. Show your respect for fish
       so favored by their lord.

31　You'd like to see your name among my lines;
　　it might redound to your credit. I don't mind
　　at all; I'd really like to put you down here.
　　But what a name: Hippodameia! I can't go around
　　saying Hippodameia all the time; how would that sound?
　　I wish Domitia Caballina—or whatever your mother uses
　　for a name—hadn't been so deaf to the Muses
　　as to crown you with a name Melpomene refuses
　　to entertain in her ear; and Polyhymnia won't say it
　　in the same breath with Apollo, or lay it
　　alongside Calliope. So take another name we'd rather
　　record, woman. We can't have you Riding Roman.

32　The bee in amber,
　　entombed in a bead of nectar,
　　lies immured in the splendor
　　of his life's labors as a collector.

33　Your bookcases are crammed with manuscripts
　　of the things you have labored to write
　　and never bothered to publish. "Oh, my heirs
　　will bring out my stuff in due course."
　　Isn't it time you perished and published?

34　That toga is far from clean;
　　like snow, it's light and thin.

35　We watched two timid does plunge
　　at each other with lowered heads
　　and sink down in mutual death.

Our hounds just stared at the loot;
it dawned on the arrogant hunter
that no work was left for his knife.
How could such placid hearts
heat up with hate like that?
Bulls charge, men kill, like that.

36   Your beard is white but your hair is black.
     I suppose you can't dye the stuff down below.

37   "Let's see now: 100,000 coming in
     from Coranus; and another 200,000
     is owed me by Marcinus, and Titus
     owes me 600,000, Sabinus a million,
     and Serranus another million.
     My apartments in town and my country places
     net me a round three million;
     and my prize sheep at Parma bring in 600,000."
     Every day you din these figures into my ear,
     and I know the sounds better than my own name.
     You ought to pay out some other line
     to keep me hooked, or salve my bruised ear
     with a sound I'd rather hear, like money
     for me. My stomach won't let me
     audit your accounts any longer, except for a fee.

38   Say you won't, Galla: For passion cloys
     if its joys are not tormenting.
     But don't take too long in relenting!

39   You buy up all sorts of silver plate:
       sole owner of authentic Myrons;
       sole owner of the handmade work
       of Praxiteles and Scopas;
       sole owner of embossed work
       from the burin of Phidias;
       sole possessor of Mentor's work.
       And you are not without some Gratians
       and Galician metal vases, gold-inlaid,
       or embossed ewers handed down in your family.
       Seeing you in the middle of all this chased metal,
       Charinus, I'm astonished to see you so tarnished.

40   When the Hall of the Pisos proudly displayed
       its rows of ancestral busts, and the famous family
       of the three Senecas still enjoyed prestige, even then
       I chose you, Postumus, above monarchs and magnates.
       You were a Knight, and not a rich one; but to me
       you were the Consul. Some thirty winters we shared
       between us as we did our bed and board.
       Now you are gorged with recognition and wealth
       in a position to bestow, no, lavish gifts
       on your friends. It's your move. But you don't.
       It's late in the game for me to go out and find
       another patron. Goddess of Fortune, what happened?
       "Oh, I meant to tell you: Postumus got away from me."

41   About to recite, with a wool scarf around your throat?
       Wouldn't it be smarter to pull the wool over our ears?

42   My ideal slave would be like this, Flaccus:
Born in Egypt—the banks of the Nile are littered
with better stuff of this sort than any other place—
but white, and shining all the fairer among
the dusky mobs of lower Egypt for being so rare.
His eyes should rival the gleaming stars;
and let the long soft hair lightly caress his neck.
I detest curly hair, Flaccus. As for the forehead,
not too high; and then, a nice little nose
set off by the curve of the nostrils; the red lips
could put to shame the dark red roses of Paestum.
When I am reluctant he ought to coax me on
and when I am ardent he ought to hold me off,
exercising more freedom than his master.
He should keep away from other boys; and push
the girls away from his door. For everyone else
a grown man and only for me the still essential boy.
"That description fits somebody I know;
it's the image of my own slave, Amazonicus."

43   Well no, Coracinus, I didn't call you a fairy—
I'd never be so brazen or quite so willing
to tell a lie. If I called you that
let the cups of Pontia and Metilus
overflow with poison for me. I swear,
by all the fanatics of Isis and Osiris,
I'm not so wild as that. I merely referred
to an insignificant well-known fact
and one you wouldn't deny, when I
said you like to get your licks in with *ladies*.

44   Only a short while ago old smoky Vesuvius
      bore a green burden of vineyards on his shoulders
and the vats below were clogged with gorgeous grapes.

This was a place whose forests high in the air
meant more to Bacchus than his Nysean hills.
  And only a short while ago Satyrs led their troupes
down this same mountainside. Here were Venus' haunts
  more appealing to her than Sparta.
And this whole landscape knew the sound of Hercules'
  roving name. He too made it holy.
    And now, there it lies submerged in ashes,
crumpled, shorn by the flames,
so curiously at odds
with the will of the gods.

45   Apollo, his majesty's Secretary Parthenius
      offers this box of gifts to you, in honor
      of his son Burrus, who this day rounds out
      his first five years. May you grant him
      round after round of Olympic cycles!
      May you take notice of his father's prayer!
      Then your laurel will love you loyally,
      your sister may cherish chastity unchallenged
      and you will shine in the splendor of youth
      everlasting. Bacchus' beautifully flowing
      tresses will grow no more luxuriantly
      than thine!

46   Winter holiday presents for Sabellus,
      an avalanche—
      no wonder he's proud of himself.
      He can't imagine another lawyer—
      to state the case clearly—
      better off than he is.
      Sabellus' disdainful pride is based on:
      half a quart of flour and dried beans,
      three half-pound containers of incense and pepper,

Lucanian sausages, Faliscan tripe,
a flask of black boiled Syrian wine,
a jar of fig jelly from Libya,
and with it, a bunch of onions,
a fistful of snails, and a wedge of cheese.
A client from Picenum
sent along a tiny basket with a few olives in it
and seven cups crudely carved in relief:
the finished work of a potter of Saguntum,
masterpieces in silver turned on some Spanish wheel;
and a napkin with a broad purple border, for fringeship.
A Saturnalia generouser than here displayed
Sabellus hasn't seen in a whole decade.

47   Here's a painting of Phaethon
executed in encaustic.
You burn the boy all over again.

48   You like to be beaten, but when it's done
you cry, do you, Papylus? Why? When it's over
you deplore it, because you're ashamed
of the perverse pleasure that makes you fawn?
Or do you rather wish it would go right on?

49   To say that epigrams are only jokes and gags
is not to know what they are, my good friend Flaccus.
The poet is more entertaining who asks you to dine
at the cannibal board of Tereus, or describes,
oh indigestible Thyestes, your dinner party;
or, the diverting poet turns your attention away
to the mythical sight of Daedalus, fittingly typed
as the one who tailored those tender wings for his son;

or wanders off with Polyphemus, the pastoral giant
pasturing preposterous sheep. Far be it from me
to enlarge on the standard rhetorical situation
and wax eloquent in the interests of inflation.
Our Muse makes no use of the billowing robes
that stalk the figures of Tragedy. "But those poems
are what everyone praises, and adores."
I admit it, they praise them: but they read ours.

50   Why harp on the fact that I'm so old, Thais?
      One is never too old for fellaship.

51   When you were worth only six thousand
      you had yourself carried about in a chair
      borne by six men, Caecilianus.
      Now that the blind goddess has showered
      ten times as much on you, and made the seams
      of your purse split with cash, you've taken to
      going about on foot. On behalf of your just deserts
      and inestimable honors, I pray for you:
      Let the gods restore your chair.

52   Riding in that crazy goat-cart of yours, for miles,
      those stones will jog you into a good case of piles.

53   I know that man over there, you see him
      setting foot inside our sacred shrine of Pallas,
      stepping over the threshold of the temple?
      The one with the stick and knapsack
      and dirty hair, and beard down to his chest;

whose wife dresses him in a greasy gown
that with his bare feet comprises his wardrobe.
And the crowd around him gives him the meals
he has yapped for. Taken in by his looks,
you would classify him as a Cynic, no doubt.
But he's only throwing dust in our eyes,
the son of a bitch in disguise.

54   The first of your family to win the oak leaf cluster
in the games for Jupiter Capitolinus, and the privilege
of wreathing your hair with the crown, Collinus,
I warn you, don't let it go to your head.
Take each hour as your last, and make the most
of every new day you get. No one has ever managed
to stave off the three woolgathering Sisters:
They know the date that is fixed, and watch for it.
You can be richer than Crispinus,
more firm and steadfast than Thrasea,
more impressive than tony Melior:
Lachesis will still not add one inch of wool.
She unwinds her sisters' spindles:
And so your life dwindles, until you are dead.
One of the sisters always stands there to cut the thread.

55   Licianus, one of the great ones of the day,
you won't let learned Arpi take inferior rank
to fine old Caius or our native Tagus. I agree.
Let poets born in the cities of Argos chant
of Mycenae or Thebes in song, or islanders hymn
the transparent sky over Rhodes, or let the Spartans
record the nude delights of their wrestling rooms,
so dear to Leda. And as for me, a Celtiberian:
I'm not ashamed to voice in verse the syllables
staunch and stern that enhance my native land.

Bilbilis is famous for its hardy metal deposits
that produce a steely edge superior to the blades
forged by the Chalybes or in Noricum. Our Platea
holds echoing iron beneath its soil, tempered true
by the Salo's waters flowing quietly but ceaselessly.
Tutela boasts a chorus, as does Rixamae, and Carduae
has handsome festivals. Peteris could be famous
for its glowing rosebushes, and Rigae
has an old time rural theater on its natural slopes.
I could mention the men of Sila sure and sharp
with their javelins, or describe the lakes
of Turgontum and Perusia and the clear calm waters
of tiny Tuetonissa; the sacred oaks at Buradon,
a grove the laziest stroller likes to roam in;
or the sloping sides of the valley of Vativesca
which Manlius plows with a brace of sturdy bullocks.
Perhaps you're smiling at these back country names,
fastidious reader? But these are the local places
I prefer to forgotten villages like Butunti.

56   And so I am meant to call you munificent
      because you lavish gifts on old men and widows?
      But, Gargilianus, that is not a generous act;
      it's a grubby thing to do and casts a dirty reflection
      on a donor like you who calls his traps gifts.
      So the crooked hook entices the hungry fish
      or the clever bait take in foolish wild beasts.
      To know what it means to give — let me give you a lesson
      in generosity; if you still don't see what it is,
      Gargilianus; bestow some gifts on me.

57   Here I sit in the lap of luxury
      beside the waters of Baiae
      and the Lucrine breakwater — off in the hills
      are grottoes glowing with subterranean heat.

You inhabit the kingdom of Tivoli
founded by a refugee from Argos
at the twentieth milestone from the city of Rome.
The time is the Sign of the Shaggy Lionheart;
Baiae blazes with more than underground warmth.
So long, holy fountains and charming brooksides,
dwellings of nymphs and naiads. You held the hills
where Hercules strode, in the frosty season, but now
give way to the chilly heights of Tivoli.

58   Galla, in mourning for your husband in seclusion?
Ashamed to show your grief outright? The conclusion
I draw is: Your husband was an illusion.

59   A viper was sliding along the branches
of a gummy poplar tree when the juicy drops
of amber enveloped the wild thing struggling
to wriggle free. Unbelieving, he watched himself
becoming enshrouded in the cloud of viscous dew
and ended up fixed fast inside the congealed gum.
Now, Cleopatra, dare you boast of your pyramid
when a viper lies visibly buried in a nobler tomb?

60   Now in the blazing heat we might as well escape
to Castrum, or Ardea, or any sunburnt landscape,
since Curiatius has laid a curse
on the air of Tivoli by dying there,
where the waters are also salubrious.
No place can fend off death. It's no worse
to expire in sickly Sardinia than in a spa.

61   Quite a setup, eh Mancinus? I hear you
      saying how so-and-so settled 200,000 on you
      just a day or so ago. Now it's the fourth session
      of our discussion at the Poets' School
      since you reminded us of those fine cloaks
      Pampulla picked out for you at a mere 10,000.
      And your girl friends snow you with jewels,
      a real sardonyx, an opal, and two emeralds.
      Yesterday, ducking out of the theater, in the middle
      of Pollio's aria, you told us on the run
      that 300,000 had just come your way in the form
      of a legacy, and this morning you mentioned
      another 100,000, and this afternoon another.
      What on earth have we done to provoke
      such a heartless humor in you? Can't you
      show some consideration and just stop talking?
      Or if your tongue won't stay still, why not wrap it
      around a subject better tuned to our ears,
      for example, you've decided to set us up with . . .

62   Black Lycoris settled in White Sulphur Springs,
      thinking anything might, at that source, turn white.

63   While a mother, Cerellia, was crossing the channel
      from Bauli to Baiae, she was drowned in the criminal
      waves. What a chance you missed there to play the hero,
      oh waters that refused to execute the orders of Nero!

64   Julius Martial's pretty little place
      lies along the long profile
      of the Janiculan Hill,
      a spot more blessed than the gardens of the Hesperides.

Broad terraces step up the hillside
to the level summit of rolling land
that breathes a purer air
and gleams in a marvelous light
above the clouds settling
on the sloping valleys below.
The shapely peaks of the villa's high roofs
verge delicately on the crystal stars.

From here you can see the seven great hills,
and drink in the total view of Rome,
as well as the Alban Hills
and the slopes of Tusculum.
You make out the cool retreats just beyond the city:
old Fidenae, and tiny Saxa Rubra,
and the sacred orchard surrounding
the spring that spurts from the ground
where Anna Perenna shed her virgin blood.

Off in the distance lie the Via Flaminia
and the Via Salaria, where the wagon drivers
sit athwart their carts, but you can't hear the sound,
no creak of wheels that could jostle you out of sleep.
You rest undisturbed by the rowers' chant
or the noisy bargemen, here, near though you are
to the Milvian Bridge, and the barges
gliding down the sacred Tiber.

The master of this country house,
or town house, if you will,
makes his dwelling all the more appealing
by making you utterly at home:
You'd think it was yours—
the whole place is yours for the asking—
you imagine you're in Alcinous' chateau—
or enjoying the hospitality
usually offered to Hercules
by those he dropped in on.

Any of you who think this isn't so much
are welcome to hack away
with a hundred hoes at your country estate

on the soil of chilly Tivoli or frosty Praeneste,
or can sign up a single farmer
to work at remote Seti, perched
on the edge of its steep rockface:
I prefer, to all that space,
Julius Martial's pretty little place.

65   Philaenis always cries in only one eye.
You ask why? She only has one eye.

66   Linus, you have always lived
a small town life,
the cheapest existence there is.
For the occasional Ides or Kalends
you chalk your modest toga,
and one outfit
sees you through ten summers.
The forests and meadows
supply the boar and hare
you don't have to pay for.
A fluttering tree furnishes you thrushes.
Fish float in from rivers and are trapped in your pools.
A red flask pours you out nonimported wine.
Your servant boy is not some effeminate chap
from somewhere in Greece, but any one in the group
of homespun kids hanging around waiting to wait on
    you.
When you're in the mood, you can have a session
with your housekeeper, or with some farmer's wife.
The midsummer heat hasn't ruined your house or your
    land,
and your merchant ship has not gone down at sea.
Why gamble for cash when you can play checkers?
And your rolling bones gather no loss.

So tell me, where is that ten million
your parsimonious mother left you?
You've run through it? In view of the circumstances,
how could you do it?

67   Hard-up Gaurus was asking a praetor for money,
on the basis of a long-standing friendship, the 100,000
he lacked to bring the 300,000 he had
to the sum he needed to qualify as a Knight,
and greet the Emperor as a legal member of that order.
The praetor said, "You know I'm due to pay
the chariot drivers Scorpus and Thallus,
and how I wish that were a matter of a mere
100,000."
Your ill-gotten-gainful, forgetful-of-past-favors
cashbox ought to be blushing by now, Praetor:
Bestowing on a horse what you refuse a Knight.

68   My meal was cheap, yours was far superior:
Was I your dinner guest, or your inferior?

69   You serve wine in the very best bottles, Papylus,
but they say the wine is not exactly the best,
they say you've become a widower four times now
thanks to those very bottles.
What a crock!
You know I wouldn't take stock
in a rumor like that, Papylus.
It's just that I'm not thirsty.

70   When his father died, Ammianus inherited
      one length of rope.
      Surprising, isn't it, to think of Ammianus
      wishing his father were still alive
      and kicking?

71   I've searched the whole city
      to find a girl who'd say No.
      There's not a girl who says No:
      It's as though
      you couldn't say No,
      it just wasn't done,
      not right, don't you know?
      And so
      not a girl
      says No.
      And so, you mean
      there's not a chaste girl to be seen?
      Heavens, there are thousands of them.
      But how do they work that out?
      They never say No,
      But then, they never give out.

72   You want copies of my books, as many
      as I have? I haven't got any.
      Tryphon the bookseller, he's the man
      with copies of my books, for cash.
      "You expect me to pay for trash
      like yours while I still have my wits about me?
      I'm not such a pushover."
      Me either.

73   Vestinus lay at death's doors,
living his last hour,
about to embark on the waters
of the Styx. He implored the daughters
of death, the dreadful Fates
who were spinning the ultimate plaits
of wool allotted to him, to do him
one final favor and grant a reprieve
of several hours in which to achieve
a piece of unfinished business: He would leave
his wealth well distributed in his will.
For you I am as good as dead, he argued,
so let me live this much longer for my friends.
Such a prayer could hardly anger even gloomy god-
    desses,
and they granted him a few hours more.
He made an ample division of his resources
and left the light well satisfied with the stage
of life he had reached, a ripe old age.

74   The amphitheater: See how the lust of battle
is caught by timid does. How can anger
grow huge in the hearts of these mild wild beasts?
Look, they're aflame to lock horns in a struggle
to the death, oh Caesar, would you come
to their help? Let the hounds loose;
with a yelp
they'll have these deer on the run.

75   Nigrina, fortunate in character,
and fortunate in your husband,
entitled you are to the highest rank
among the married daughters of Latium.

It has been your pleasure to confer
on your husband the wealth your father
settled on you. You are happy in sharing
your money as well as your life
on equal terms with him.
Evadne hurled herself on the funeral pyre
to join her husband in the final flames.
Immortal fame bore Alcestis off in death
to glory under the stars.
You have done better by far:
In fulfilling your vow here above,
you need not die to prove
your love.

76   When I asked you for twelve you sent six,
     so I'm in a fix. But when I need more,
     say twelve, oh I know. . . . I'll say twenty-four.

77   Never have I dunned the gods for money,
     satisfied with my lot,
     contented with my little.
     But now, Poverty, Honey,
     get thee behind me, if you don't mind.
     And what's my reason for this new angle
     on prayer? I want to make Zoilus
     so jealous he'll strangle.

78   You've seen your sixtieth harvest,
     your face gleams under a mass of white hair,
     but you still race all over town.
     There isn't a couch adorned with a noble matron
     that doesn't hear the nervous echo
     of your early morning "Good Morning, How Are You?"

A Tribune can't budge without your being beside him
to escort him out of the house,
neither Consul can make a decision
without the benefit of your thinking.
Ten times a day
you puff up the Sacred Way
to the imperial Palatine,
constantly dropping the names
of Sigerus, the Chamberlain,
and Parthenius, the First Secretary.
You curry favor strategically
the way young men energetically
ought to, but on you such frenetically
ardent morning strife is unbecoming,
Afer, old boy.
Nothing is so out of place
as an old man, unwanted, living
at such a frantic pace.

79   A frequent guest in my villa at Tivoli,
      you've gone and bought it. How silly of me,
      to impose on you by selling you your own home.

80   Reciting in public when running a fever
      is madness, Maron. You're delirious. You're not serious?
      You declaim when you're sick, you declaim before rows
      of seats when you have a tertian. Of course, I suppose,
      if there's no other way to work up a sweat,
      and yet. . . .
      "But it's important." Wrong! When fever's running riot
      in your bones, it's important to keep quiet.

81   Fabulla read the epigram wherein I complain
      that there's not a girl around here who says No.
      And so when asked the first time, she refused;
      and the second time, and the third, she declined.
      But Fabulla, say you won't thwart all endeavor:
      I told you just to say No, not Never.

82   Oh Rufus, please say a word for Books III and IV
      to Venuleius; charge my account with an hour or more
      of idle indulgence. I hope he can take his mind off his
         troubles
      and work for a moment, and turn a kind ear to these
         baubles
      of mine. I'd like to know what he thinks.
      Right in the middle of the drinks,
      not after the first round, or after the last,
      but in congenial Bacchus' mid-flight.
      Maybe two is too many, so make a tight
      roll of one and his reading will look light.

83   When you feel free and confident
      there's no one more hateful,
      when you are worried and shaky
      there's no one more attractive.
      When you're secure you won't return
      anyone's greeting, you snub us all,
      you're the only free citizen on earth.
      When you're nervous, you generously share
      whatever you have, and greet us first
      and say Sir and Mister. To serve us
      well, Naevolus, go on being nervous.

84   Not a man in town will say
          he's fucked Thais. But lots
          like her and keep after her.
          So she's chaste? Oh no, barefaced.

85   We drink from a glass, you from opaque spar.
          Why? So the translucence won't jar
          when we compare the two kinds of wine?

86   If you want the acclaim
          of critical Athenian ears, book, aim
          at the learned Apollinaris.
          If you find you are in his
          good graces, cast your worries aside.
          There is none whose learning's more wide
          or deep, or any more demanding.
          And yet he is understanding,
          and congenial and honest, and right.
          If he finds you rather a delight
          and quotes you, you won't lose heart
          if meaner men tear you apart,
          nor submit in your execution tunic,
          smeared with pitch and resin, as the tonic
          treatment for grocers who wish
          to use your leaves to wrap fish.
               But if he finds fault with your lines,
               you'll end up in the confines
               of some salt-fish seller who'll buy
               you up cheap for his paper supply.
                    Or, schoolkids can plough your unwritten side,
                    with their scrawling pens, and take it out on
                      your hide.

87   Your Bassa, Fabullus, cuddles that baby
and takes it everywhere, hugs it to her heart,
calls it cute names. Because she adores babies?
No, just that she often has to fart.

88   You didn't send me any gift
in return for my modest one to you,
and the Saturnalia is through.
Not even six ounces of silver,
from Septicianus' worst specimens.
Not even a drab linen napkin,
the token dab of a grouchy client.
Nothing reached me, not even
some tuna fishes from Antibes
in a little red pot. A small jar
of figs from Syria? Not what I got!
How inferior of me to miss out on that lot.
Or how about just a flat
little bag of wrinkled olives from Picenum?
I never even seen 'em, much less sunk
a tooth in 'em. I didn't see none,
not one, any one
of which would entitle you to say
you'd remembered me on the holiday.
You can fool other people that way,
with your wide smile and warm handshake,
but I know you now, you big fake.

89   Hold it, book, that's enough!
We've come to the knob at the end of the roll.
You object? And want to keep going right on
and can't sit still cooped up in the last column

on the last leaf? As though for you the work wasn't done
that was done when the first page was over and gone.
Your reader is tired, he's getting gruff,
the bookseller is losing interest in your stuff:
Hold it, book, that's enough!

NOTES

The Book of the Games

EPIGRAM 1 *Apollo's Altar*   An altar allegedly made by Apollo (when four years old) from the horns of animals slain by Diana.

Mausoleum   The tomb of Mausolus, ruler of Caria in Asia Minor, 377–353 B.C., erected at Halicarnassus by his widow Artemisia.

The Flavian Amphitheater   The "Colosseum," begun by Vespasian and completed by Titus, on the low ground formerly used by Nero as a huge private pond in the architectural complex of his Golden House. Nero had also included in the Golden House setting a 100-foot statue of himself (the *Colossus Neronis*—rivaling the Colossus of Rhodes, a bronze statue of the Sun-God). Vespasian had the head of Nero taken off this statue and replaced by an image of the Sun crowned with seven rays, and had the statue moved to a position on the Sacred Way. In epigram 70 of Book I Martial mentions that his messenger will be dazzled by the "Colossus" as he turns up the Sacred Way ascending the Palatine:

> Nec te detineat miri radiata colossi
> quae Rhodium moles vincere gaudet opus.

Hadrian, in the process of constructing the vast platform for his double temple of Venus and Rome, had the statue moved again (the maneuver requiring the use of 24 elephants), and placed near the north entrance of the Flavian Amphitheater. From this final juxtaposition the arena took its popular name, the Colosseum.

199

EPIGRAM 4   *That huge gang. . . . expenses*   In ruling out the use of "informers," *delatores*, Titus also of course lost the income derived from confiscating the estates of those they denounced!

EPIGRAM 5   *Pasiphae*   Of Nero's theatrical compulsions in the year 58 A.D., Suetonius writes: "He also exhibited a naval battle in salt water with sea monsters swimming about in it; besides pyrrhic dances by some Greek youths, handing each of them certificates of Roman citizenship at the close of his performance. The pyrrhic dances represented various scenes. In one a bull mounted Pasiphae, who was concealed in a wooden image of a heifer; at least many of the spectators thought so. Icarus at his very first attempt fell close by the imperial couch and bespattered the emperor with his blood; for Nero very seldom presided at the games, but used to view them while reclining on a couch, at first through small openings, and then with the entire balcony uncovered."
The Lives of the Caesars "Nero" XII, 2, tr. Rolfe (Loeb, II, p. 105)

EPIGRAM 12   *Lucina*   An aspect of Diana, deity of the chase and of childbirth.

EPIGRAM 33   *third issue*   As a denunciation of Domitian, this epigram would not have appeared until after his death in 96 and so does not form a part of the original group of poems in the *liber spectaculorum*.

Book I

EPIGRAM 2   *Temple of Peace*   dedicated by Vespasian in 75 A.D. after celebrating the capture of Jerusalem.

    Transitorium   Also called the Palladium or Forum of Pallas, containing a temple of Athena; begun by Domitian and completed by Nerva.

EPIGRAM 3   *Argiletum*   Most bookstores and many other small shops were situated on this street at the north end of the Forum Romanum.

EPIGRAM 7   *Stella*   L. Arruntius Stella of Patavium (Padua), a patron and friend of Martial and Statius.

EPIGRAM 8   *Decianus*   From Emerita (Merida) in Spain, one of Martial's closest friends in Rome.

EPIGRAM 12   *Regulus*   M. Aquilius Regulus, a famous lawyer and a notorious *delator* under Nero and Domitian. He became very rich.

EPIGRAM 13   *Arria and Paetus*   Caecina Paetus, arrested and condemned to death for conspiring against Claudius, was advised by his wife Arria to commit suicide. She set him the example by stabbing herself first and handing him the sword.

EPIGRAM 15   *Julius Martial*   For thirty-three years one of the poet's closest friends.

EPIGRAM 16   *Avitus*   Stertinius Avitus, Consul in 92 A.D. He had a bust of Martial in his library, for which Martial wrote the inscription:

> Ille ego sum nulli nugarum laude secundus
>   quem non miraris sed puto lector amas.
> Maiores maiora sonent: mihi parva locuto
>   sufficit in vestras saepe redire manus.

> Lo! he am I whose light verse yields to none;
> Reader, thy love, not awe methinks I've won.
> Let greater men strike greater notes: I earn
> Enough if my small themes oft to thy hands return.

Prefatory epistle of Book IX, tr. by Ker (Loeb, II, p. 69).

EPIGRAM 21   *hand*   The young Gaius Mucius "Scaevola" volunteered to enter the Etruscan camp and assassinate the king Lars Porsenna who was besieging Rome. Uncertain which was the king and afraid of giving himself away in the crowd by asking, Mucius struck the king's secretary. When caught and condemned to death, Mucius held his right hand in the sacrificial coals until it burned off and showed no signs of fear or pain. Lars Porsenna was so impressed by this act of self-control that he set Mucius free and lifted the siege. The story is told in Livy's *History*, Book II, chapters 12–14.

EPIGRAM 36   *Curvii*   Lucanus and Tullus Curvius, two brothers of aristocratic rank, types of fraternal affection.

EPIGRAM 49   *Licianus*   Like Martial, born at Bilbilis.

EPIGRAM 55   *Fronto*   A distinguished lawyer and soldier.

EPIGRAM 59   *gloomy baths of Lupus and Gryllus*   Privately owned bathing establishments less showy than the public baths named for Emperors.

EPIGRAM 70   As landmarks on the walk through the Forum Romanum along the Sacred Way to the Palatine hill Martial refers to the Temple of Castor and Pollux, the House of the Vestal Virgins, the Colossus Neronis, and on the Palatine to a temple of Bacchus and of Cybele the Great Mother (Magna Mater).

EPIGRAM 87   *Cosmus*   A fashionable *parfumeur*.

EPIGRAM 96   *scazon* "The hobbler," an iambic trimeter verse with a trochee replacing the iambus in the last foot. The last two feet are like the metrical unit called the choliambus: ⌣ – – ⌣ .

EPIGRAM 105   *Ovid*   Not the Augustan poet but Quintus Ovidius, Martial's friend and neighbor at Nomentum, a small town 14½ miles northeast of Rome.

Go, lovely rose

Apollinaris   Domitius Apollinaris, a friend of Martial.

Book II

EPIGRAM 2   *Domitianus Germanicus*   Domitian assumed the name Germanicus in 84 after his victory over the Chatti (Hessians).

EPIGRAM 14   *portico . . . Europa*   A colonnade in the Campus Martius built by Agrippa's sister and decorated with paintings of the rape of Europa.

              Voting District . . . Portico of Chiron . . . Jason   The Saepta Julia, in the Campus Martius once used as a voting place, now a shopping center and meeting place. Among its statuary was a group depicting the centaur Chiron and his ward Achilles. The frescoes of Jason and the Argonauts were part of a neighboring colonnade, the *Porticus Argonautarum.*

Realm of Isis and Serapis   There was a temple to these Egyptian deities in the Campus Martius with a large expanse of lawn in the forecourt.

Hecatonstylon   A long, roofed arcade with 100 columns built by Pompey and near the Colonnade and Theater of Pompey.

EPIGRAM 17   *Subura Street . . . bloodstained scourges*   Subura: "a quarter in Rome between the Esquiline, Viminal, and Quirinal, where provisions were sold and where many prostitutes dwelt" (Lewis & Short, *A Latin Dictionary*). Subura Street was a continuation of the Argiletum leading to the Esquiline. The "scourges" were the whips used by public executioners and hung up on a pike or displayed high on a wall to impress the passers-by.

EPIGRAM 59   *Mica*   "The Tiny," a banquet hall of Domitian with a view on the Mausoleum of Augustus.

EPIGRAM 89   *Apicius*   M. Gabius Apicius, the famous gourmand.

EPIGRAM 90   *Quintilian*   M. Fabius, born at Calagurris in Spain. Quintilian held the chair of rhetoric founded by Vespasian, presiding over Roman letters authoritatively from 69–89 A.D.

EPIGRAM 91   *"father of three children"*   Both Titus and Domitian conferred the privileges legislated in the form of the *Ius Trium Liberorum* on Martial. The income and rank (membership in the Equestrian Order) derived from this official status could be given to parents without issue and to single men.

Meno Rumore!

Colchian incantations   Apotropaic clashing of brass gongs to drive away the evil demons during an eclipse (attributed to witches), devised by the Colchian priesthood.

Sulpicia's Poems

Sulpicia   A poetess of the time about whom no more is known than is said here by Martial, although she is mentioned later by Ausonius and Sidonius.

Phaon   Allegedly the inamorato of Sappho.

Book III

EPIGRAM 1   *Gallia Togata*   Not actually "Provence" as I have translated it here, but that provincial territory in northern Italy south of the Alps extending roughly from Savoie to the Tyrol.

EPIGRAM 4   *Via Aemilia . . . Forum Cornelii*   The Via Aemilia ran from Ariminum (Rimini) to Placentia (Piacenza). Forum Cornelii, named after the dictator Sulla, is the modern Imola.

EPIGRAM 5   *First House*   Literally *primae . . . in limine tectae*, i.e. near the Covered Way, a colonnade closed at both ends near the Mausoleum of Augustus.

EPIGRAM 47   *Porta Capena*   The gate leading to the Via Appia.

Book IV

EPIGRAM 3   *Caesar's son*   An allusion to Domitian's son who died in infancy and was deified.

EPIGRAM 11   *Saturninus*   In 88 A.D. Lucius Antonius Saturninus had two legions of the Rhine contingent proclaim him emperor and sought the alliance of the Germans. Norbanus crushed this revolt. Saturninus' name Antonius recalls the name of Mark Antony.

EPIGRAM 13   *Pudens*   Aulus Pudens of Sarsina in Umbria, friend of Martial, and a centurion.

EPIGRAM 14   *C. Silius Italicus*   Famous orator, lawyer and poet. Consul in 68 A.D. and Pro-Consul of Asia, the author of a long epic poem, *The Punica*, on the Second Punic War.

EPIGRAM 22   *Cleopatra*   Not the queen of Egypt, but an attractive Roman wife.

EPIGRAM 25   *Altinum*   In the region of Venetia. In legend Phaethon fell to earth there. Sola was the nymph-spirit of the Euganean Lake (modern La Solana) who married Faunus, the deity of the River Po.

Aquileia   A legendary tradition was that the Argo floated on the Timavus River from Aquileia to the Adriatic. The region would therefore have been one honored by Castor and Pollux (the sons of Leda) and Cyllarus, Pollux' mythical steed.

BIBLIOGRAPHICAL NOTE

The Loeb Classical Library two-volume edition of Martial's epigrams, with Latin text and English translation by Walter C. A. Ker (1920) contains useful notes and a valuable Index of Proper Names and Index of First Lines. In this edition the obscene epigrams are translated by the Italian of Graglia (London, 1782), as is also the practice in the Bohn Classical Library edition (London, 1897), a collection of prose and verse translations by various hands. Modern verse translations of selected epigrams have been made by Rolfe Humphries (Indiana University Press, 1963), Dudley Fitts (Harcourt, Brace and World, 1967) and Philip Murray (Wesleyan University Press, 1967).

The account of Martial's life and work in J. W. Duff, *A Literary History of Rome*, Vol. II, is still very serviceable. Gaston Boissier's essay in *Tacitus and Other Roman Studies* (New York, 1906) is lively and interesting. Paul Nixon's *Martial and the Modern Epigram* (ca. 1930) is an amusing book comparing Martial and other epigrammatists. The best book available on Martial is the study of Luigi Pepe, *Marziale*, (Naples, 1950), in Italian.